by Darylann Whitemarsh

HANNIBAL BOOKS
Hannibal, Missouri—"America's Home Town"
(Use coupon in back to order extra copies of this and other
helpful books from Hannibal Books.)

HANNIBAL BOOKS
Hannibal, Missouri—"America's Home Town"
(Use coupon in back to order extra copies of this and other
helpful books from Hannibal Books.)

THANK YOU!

To Jill Wilson of Moody Monthly magazine for planting the seed.
To talented Lila Shelburne for editing the manuscript.
To the people who encouraged, prayed, and supported me during this project.
A SPECIAL THANK YOU TO: Dr. James Hefley, whose writing expertise, hours of listening and encouragement and dedication to helping Christian writers made this book posssible.

Table of Contents

"All that is necessary for the triumph of evil is for good men to do nothing."
Edmund Burke

Chapter 1

The Alarm Bells Are Ringing

Listen up, folks.

Hear Billy Graham: "We're in a state of war between good and evil. America is in a battle for survival.[1]"

The alarm bells are ringing. The sirens are sounding. The red lights are flashing from Maine to California, warning of calamity unless America is changed.

The long and short of it is that we must start now if America is to be changed and pulled back from the brink.

Stop, Look, Listen!

Our government—that's us—now owes three trillion (three thousand billion!) dollars. Much of this money is owed to foreigners. We are sinking into a financial morass.

Foreigners now own many of the largest "American" corporations. For example, an Arab investment conglomerate recently purchased the Saks-Fifth Avenue chain of stores. The Japanese are whipping us in the world market and taking thousands of jobs from Americans.

Wall Street crooks have stolen tens of billions of dollars in illegal trading. The savings and loan scandals may cost the public treasury a trillion dollars. Add more billions for scandals in the Department of Housing and Urban Development.

Our government has been caught using citizen tax money to fund despicable pornography and obscenity. Our taxes helped pay for "art" depicting anal sex, lesbian oral sex, a man urinating into the mouth of another, nude children in suggestive poses, a crucifix in urine, and other offensive drawings and photos—more than enough to make Nero blush.

You can see stuff almost as bad on TV, including homosexuals cavorting in bed and actors and actresses involved in incestual relationships. Commercials from "respectable" companies, whose products we buy, keep such trash on the air.

Homosexual marriage is close to being legalized in many cities. A Massachusetts Congressman admits to having homosexual relations with a teenager, and—guess what? The people in his district keep re-electing him.

Two-hundred and sixty different "kiddie porn" magazines circulate around the country. That's titles, not the total number of issues. Hard core pornography depicting child molestation, bestiality, and almost every imaginable form of perversion has become a multi-billion dollar business.

Satanic cults are increasing. In one incident, a devil cult sacrificed and apparently cannibalized 12 people, including a college student on spring break.

Listen up, please. Sorry to spoil your dinner, but you need to hear more that will make you angry enough to want to get involved.

Twenty-four million babies have been murdered since the Supreme Court made baby killing legal. Over one and one-half million sweet little unborn babies will die in licensed death chambers this year.

The sexual activity of teenage girls has increased five-fold since 1960 from an estimated 10 to 50 percent of the population. More than one million teens get pregnant each year. In one large city over 70 percent of the babies are born out of wedlock.

The deadly AIDS epidemic—principally caused by homosexual sex—is sweeping the country. Sixty percent of the babies born in the New York Bronx have AIDS.

A thousand babies are born to drug addicts every day. They are doomed to be addicts themselves.

The rate of teenage suicides has almost doubled in the past nine years. Youth suicide is especially high among teens who fear they might have homosexuals tendencies.

And by the way, a government publication blames church teaching that homosexuality is wrong for many of these suicides. The government writer says Biblical teaching has made gays feel guilty. What gall!

Again, I plead, listen up.

While freedom of religious expression is increasing in Eastern Europe and the Soviet Union, it appears to be decreasing in America. A court recently ordered a Colorado teacher to remove a Bible from his private classroom library. Another court ruled that passengers bound for Christmas flights at O'Hare Airport in Chicago can listen to "Jingle Bells," but not "Silent Night." Still another judge in Kentucky decreed that the Ten Commandments must be removed from the walls of state schools.

Please, please get this.

"Family" is being redefined in public school textbooks to mean, "Two or more persons who share resources, share responsibility for decisions, share values and goals, and have a commitment to one another over time."[2] Under that definition almost any group living together, including homosexuals, can qualify for government family benefits.

Immoral sex education parades under the guise of "health studies" in many schools, with traditional morality stripped from the curriculum. The idea is to teach children "safe sex," not abstinence. Children are told that "homosexuals can lead lives that are as full and healthy as those of heterosexuals."[3] And that "men and women are more free to do [sexually] and be whatever feels comfortable for them."[4]

Please, please, don't run and hide.

Crime is rampant. Prisons are overcrowded in almost every state. In most cities it is unsafe to walk the downtown streets after dark, and even in the daytime in some urban areas.

Crime among lawyers has also increased. That should come as no surprise since law schools no longer require courses in the foundations of morality.

Do Any Americans Have Values Anymore?

From what you read, see, and hear in the media, you'd think only a few people practice traditional, Judeo-Christian morality anymore, and that few people bother to attend church today. Have you ever, even once, seen a contemporary evangelical Christian character honestly portrayed on TV? Notice I said "contemporary," for it's okay to show Christians (as in "The Waltons" and "Little House on the Prairie," for example) as they were 50-100 years ago.

This is because the secular mass media reflects the movers, makers, and shakers in mass communications and the entertainment world.

A team of sociologists from George Washington University interviewed 240 of the major news media elite and found:

- Only one out of ten admitted attending any recent religious services.
- Nine out of ten favored legalized abortion.
- Ninety-one percent saw nothing wrong with homosexual practices.
- More than 50 percent said adultery was okay.

The researchers received similar answers when they interviewed graduate students in journalism at Columbia University and TV and film leaders in New York and Los Angeles.

Contrast this with findings of a 1989 Gallup Poll that surveyed a scientific sample of all Americans.

At least half said they attended a church or synagogue each week.

Seventy-eight percent did not favor greater sexual freedom.

A large majority approved stronger family ties and more emphasis on hard work.[5]

Other polls show similar contrasts between the beliefs and practices of a secular elite and the majority of Americans.

Conclusion: There are really two "populations" in America. An elite minority in media, government, education, business, and liberal religion is leading us toward abandonment of the ideals and morals which made America great.

The majority of us are allowing this to happen. British political reformer Edmund Burke tells us why: "All that is necessary for the triumph of evil is for good men to do nothing." Let's turn this around to say: "All that is necessary for good to triumph is that moral upright men and women unite and do something."

Impossible? Not for John Wesley, who led a moral and spiritual revival in the 18th century that saved England from bloody revolution. Nor for Jonathan Edwards, who sparked the "Great Awakening" which purified and prepared America for the fight for independence.

I hear a Christian brother or sister saying, "This is to be expected in the last days. The reign of evil is a sure sign that Jesus is coming soon. There is nothing we can do, except to wait for His return."

Pardon me, but that's a copout. I, too, believe Jesus is coming, but I don't know when, and neither do you.

Aren't you glad that America's founding fathers didn't take that escape?

Another familiar excuse from duty and action is, "What can little ole me do to change America?"

History is replete with examples of "little ole me's" who did great things for God and their fellow humans.

Bob Pierce answered this excuse in asking Americans to send $10 a month for the care of war orphans in Korea. "Just because you cannot do everything, don't fail to do something," he urged. Pierce's war orphan project grew into World Vision, the greatest private Christian relief organization in the world's history.

Remember the story about the little Dutch boy who held back the sea by sticking his finger into the hole in the dike? And the little shepherd boy, David, who killed a giant with a sling shot and five smooth stones?

The excuse that "little ole me" can't do anything just won't wash.

The problem for most of us is plain old apathy. Most of us don't really get "shook up" about rampaging paganism and immorality until something hits us close to home. Our child comes home from school spouting some immoral nonsense and we get aroused. Our temperature shoots up. We get excited. We may tell somebody "off," or even write a letter to the local paper. Then we fall back and say, "Well, I took my stand. I did something."

You spoke out and that's commendable. But there's much, much more that we can do. We can be more than thermometers to "tell the temperature" of the times. We have a responsibility to be the thermostats that raise the moral and spiritual temperature of America.

In respect to public school curriculum, it's your taxes that pay the bills, your vote that helps elect the school board member in your district, and your child that attends the school. As a parent you have rights, and you can, in alliance with other concerned parents, get something done.

From "Dogbite" Cases to the Supreme Court

Maybe you're a young Christian lawyer like Michael Whitehead of Kansas City. Mike was just starting out in practice, doing "dogbite" cases, he says, when he learned that Christian students were not being allowed to meet for Bible study on the local campus of the University of Missouri. Other special interest groups, including a homosexual organization and a club of political radicals, were allowed to meet, but Christians were not.

Mike notified the university that this was a violation of free speech. When school authorities still refused to let the Christians meet, the young attorney took legal action. The case eventually went to the United States Supreme Court where a majority of justices declared the university rule unconstitutional. Thanks to Mike Whitehead and friends who supported him, Christian students now have "equal access" for their meetings on any public university or college campus in America.

The "Enlistment" Office is Open

Many of us are deeply frustrated and grieved over what the elite special interest groups are doing to destroy our society. Some of us are already in the trenches fighting for this nation and the future of our children. Some of us are bloodied and searching for better ways to win this war against immorality.

We are concerned about AIDS, pornography, abortion, drugs, crime, political corruption, and a host of other evils. We want to make America great again. We invite you to join us in making America once again the lighthouse to the world.

That's why I've written this book. I want to have a part in changing America, and I know you do too.

Stay with me for the next 12 chapters, and I believe you'll see how it can be done.

But before we consider further how we can change America, let us first try to understand where America has been and what she has become. Abraham Lincoln wisely observed, "If we know where we have been, we [can] better know where we are heading."

*"Our ancestors established their system of govern-
ment on morality and religious sentiment. Moral
habits, they believed, cannot safely be trusted on any
other foundation than religious principle, nor any
government be secure which is not supported by
moral habits."*
Daniel Webster

Chapter 2

What's Happened to the "Soul" of America?

The year is 1620. The American "dream" is in danger of
sinking as wrenching swells beat and twist the disabled
Mayflower. Suddenly, a shattering noise splits the dark,
stormy air. The ship's main deck support beam has crack-
ed. The vessel threatens to split apart and dump the
voyaging Pilgrims into the raging Atlantic. Faith fights off
panic as the crew rush to see what can be done.

"Get the screw from the printing press!" one of the
Pilgrims shouts. "It's our only hope."

Brawny men grab their tools and remove the screw.
They install it in the support beam just in time to keep the
ship from snapping in two. The sails tighten. The ship
stabilizes and plows on through the heavy seas toward the
coast of Massachusetts and the landing at Plymouth Rock.

You probably won't find in a current school history book
the story of the printing press and the screw which saved
the Pilgrims from disaster. The captain of the hired crew
had urged that the heavy press not be brought aboard. The
Pilgrims insisted that it be taken along, even though this
meant some provisions had to be left behind. The press
was to be used for printing portions of the Bible for evan-

gelization of other colonists.

The Pilgrims—whose landing Thomas Caryle calls the "beginning of the soul" of America—hoped to establish a Christian nation in the New World. So they declared in their famous Mayflower Compact: "We are knit together in a body in a most strict and sacred bond and covenant of the Lord. . . "

The covenant required all members of the colony, even non-church members who came with them, to abide by the rules agreed upon by the majority, including Sabbath keeping and honoring marriage vows.

Before constructing any homes, they built an Assembly House for meetings of the democratically elected General Court. Prayers opened every court session. Prayers are still given in the United States Congress and the Supreme Court, although secularists keep seeking to have them declared a violation of the separation of church and state.

The Founders' Vision: One Nation Under God.

The founding fathers envisioned the growth of a mighty nation under God. Governor William Bradford expressed their hope: ". . . As one small candle may light a thousand, so the light here kindled hath shown unto man, yea in some sort to our whole nation; let the glorious name of Jehovah have all the praise."[6]

Textbook writers may have changed history in today's school books, but the reality remains: Biblical teaching and ideals permeated American public life before and for many years after the Revolution. The Pilgrims didn't just "give thanks." They gave thanks "to God," which is conveniently omitted from some modern textbooks.

The three most influential 17th century leaders were Thomas Hooker, Roger Williams, and William Penn—men who would be termed evangelicals today, if not fundamentalists.

Pastor Hooker led three congregations to set up a democratic government in Connecticut. Their constitution, The Fundamental Orders of Connecticut, called for an "orderly and decent government according to God."[7] This first American constitution served as the prototype for the constitution which we revere today.

Roger Williams, the "Apostle of Religious Liberty," founded Rhode Island Colony. He opposed religious intolerance, but he never suggested (as some of his admirers do today) that God and Biblical moral values should be separated from government.

William Penn, the Quaker founder of Pennsylvania, drew up the famous "Frame of Government" which guaranteed every free man a vote and religious freedom for all. Penn said that the way to make citizens good was to convert them to Christ. Imagine the uproar if the governor of your state said that today!

The signers of the Declaration of Independence were all God-fearing men. Not one was a professing atheist, though Thomas Jefferson and several others were not orthodox Christians. Jefferson, a deist, asked for the "protection of Divine Providence" to secure the "certain unalienable rights" with which "all men are created equal" and "endowed by their Creator."[8]

America's bent for caring was born and nurtured in the revivalistic moral fervor of our early history. Church-related "funds" and "societies" bore such names as the American Female Moral Reform Society, the Association for the Relief of Respectable Aged, and the Fund for Pious Uses. From these and other Christian motivated groups came the great social concern organizations of today. The Fund for Pious Uses, for example, is the "parent" of Social Security.

A Search for America's Greatness

America, in the 19th century, was seen as the success model of the world. The famous French statesman and historian, Alexis de Tocqueville, came to discover why and wrote:

"I sought for the greatness and genius of America in her commodious harbors and her ample rivers, and it was not there.

"I sought for the greatness and genius of America in her fertile fields and boundless forests, and it was not there.

"I sought for the greatness and genius of America in her rich mines and her vast world commerce, and it was not there.

"I sought for the greatness and genius of America in her public school system and her institutions of learning, and it was not there.

"I sought for the greatness and genius of America in her democratic congress and her matchless constitution, and it was not there.

"Not until I went into the churches of America and heard her pulpits flame with righteousness did I understand the secret of her genius and power.

"America is great because America is good, and if America ever ceases to be good, America will cease to be great."[9]

What the Supreme Court Said

All the historians writing before 1960, whom I have read, agree with H.G. Wells, a skeptic, that America's founding is "indubitably Christian."[10] Supreme Court Justice William O. Douglas, a man not known for orthodox Christian beliefs, declared in 1951: "We are a religious people and our institutions presuppose a Supreme Being." Douglas largely based his conclusion upon a previous Supreme Court study that concluded, ". . . This is a Christian nation."[11]

The historical evidence cannot be disputed. The founders intended for America to be governed by Biblical principles. They believed that America had a divine purpose to fulfill. "The settlement of America," declared President John Adams, marked "the opening of a grand scheme and design in Providence for the illumination of the ignorant, and the emancipation of the slavish part of mankind all over the earth."[12]

This commonly held belief in America's "manifest destiny" endured to the mid-20th century. Now it is under siege by the gurus of popular culture who claim that the old ways are being replaced by a pluralism in which anything goes. Whatever turns you on, they say, is the "soul" of America.

"A pluralistic society like the United States cannot continue free without a shared morality. It will dissolve or be taken over by force."
Dr. John Brabner-Smith

Chapter 3

How Did We Get Into Such a Mess?

Everywhere I go, I hear people—especially those past 50—asking, "What has happened to America? How did our country get into the mess that it's now in?" How is it, for example, that in many hospitals, doctors are in one wing killing babies by abortion who are "younger" than "preemies" being saved by other doctors in another wing?

If we're going to change America, we must answer these questions. We must know the disease, if we are to find a cure.

Let's look first at what has happened in public education.

Public Education was a Christian Idea

The American public school system was founded by Christians and for over 300 years championed Biblical morality. Public schools began as Christian schools.

The Dutch Reformed Church set up the first public school in the New World in 1633. Fourteen years later, Bible-believing Puritans in Massachusetts passed a bill calling for a tax-supported public school in each township of 50 or more families—to thwart the "old Deluder," Satan. By Independence there were public schools in every state where the teacher began each day with prayer and Bible reading and taught Biblical morality.

Public schools continued to teach Biblical morality long
after Independence. The best known 19th century
textbooks were Noah Webster's Bluebacked Speller and
the McGuffey Readers. The Speller began with a prayer:

No man may put off the law of God.
My joy is in His law all the day,
O may I not go in the way of sin.
Let me not go in the way of ill men."

This is the Webster of dictionary fame. His original
dictionary is studded with Biblical expressions. Take just
two entries:

"Hope: A well founded Scriptural 'hope' is, in our
religion, the source of ineffable happiness."
"Love: The Christian 'loves' his Bible. If our hearts are
right, we 'love' God above all things."[13]

Don't bother looking for such examples in a modern
Webster's.

The author of McGuffey's Readers was a Presbyterian
minister. Packed with Biblical morals, the books were
used by three generations of Americans. Over 100 million
copies were sold.

Modern Education is "Flunking" Out

Public education has come a long way since Webster and
McGuffey. A long way in the wrong direction. Christianity
is now under attack. American heroes are ignored or
degraded. Socialism and collectivism are lauded. Parents
are put down as "old-fashioned." Morals are declared to be
relative. Sexual abstinence is excluded from sex education. Here are a few excerpts from public school textbooks
of today:

Resurrection: "A great many myths deal with the idea
of rebirth. Jesus, Dionysus, Odin, and many other traditional figures are represented as having died, after which
they were reborn, or arose from the dead."[14]

Communist hero Fidel Castro: "A practical politician
who felt securely in command, Castro frankly admitted his
mistakes. He gave the Cubans a sense of pride in the
achievements their small island-nation was making

without being tied to its powerful neighbor to the north [the U.S.]."[15]

Sexual behavior: "Adolescent petting is an important opportunity to learn about sexual response and to gratify sexual and emotional desires without a more serious commitment."[16]

Instruction from a teacher's book: "Role play being drunk and coming home to find your parents sitting in the living room with friends. How would you get past them without their knowledge?"[17]

Instruction to English teacher: "Please refrain from moralizing of any kind. Students may indeed 'tune out' if they are subjected to preachy talk about 'proper English' and the moral obligation to 'do one's best' in class and to 'lend a hand' to the underdog in a battle."[18]

What of America's universities and colleges? Virtually all of the older educational institutions owe their existence to Bible-believing church people.

Harvard was founded by Congregationalists in 1636, William and Mary by Anglicans in 1693, Yale by Congregationalists in 1701, Princeton by Presbyterians in 1746, Columbia by Anglicans in 1754, Brown by Baptists in 1765, Rutgers by Dutch Reformed in 1766, and Dartmouth by Congregationalists in 1770. The last five schools were born out of the Great Awakening revivals which preceded the fight for independence.

Higher education today (except for a few schools still closely tied to evangelical church bodies) is like the proverbial old gray mare. It isn't, by a long shot, what it used to be.

Where Have All the Values Gone?

Values have been neutralized. Coed dorms are common. Visitation rights for the opposite sex are expected. Rapes occur frequently on many campuses. At the University of Missouri young women are advised not to walk on campus alone or go to the bathroom in their dorm alone. Sex is so accepted that condom dispensers are available in lobbies and bathrooms. At Stanford University the student magazine sponsored a condom-rating contest, encouraging students to try out seven different condoms "by yourself, with a partner, or partners. Be creative. Have fun. Enjoy."[19]

Many "church" colleges have professors who mock historic Christianity. In some tax-supported state universities, professors who believe in creationism or publicly oppose abortion on demand are denied tenure. For example, Jerry Bergman, Ph.D. says he was fired from Bowling Green University in Kentucky after stating that he was a creationist. He did not teach creationism in the classroom—his doctorate is in statistics and researching. His teaching performance and scholarly writing were rated as outstanding by nine professors, but he was denied tenure after a departmental evaluation in which a single fellow professor raised questions about his religious beliefs. Dr. Bergman later noted that his chief opponent was a homosexual teacher who passed out handbills in class pushing his gay lifestyle.[20] So much for tolerance.

The shallowness of learning by many college students is appalling. A Gallup Poll found many seniors did not know that Columbus landed in the Western Hemisphere before 1500; 58 percent did not know that Shakespeare wrote The Tempest; nearly a fourth believed a famous saying by Karl Marx, "From each according to his ability, to each, according to his need," was part of the U.S. Constitution.[21]

The Foundations of Law are Crumbling

Our American founders held with Christian theologian John Calvin that the power of government to enforce law came from the Almighty. The founders saw the authority of God as expressed in the Bible as the cornerstone of an ordered, law-obeying society. The Ten Commandments were written into the legal heritage of our nation. They were not up for a Supreme Court ruling on right or wrong.

Some of our most treasured legal protections are rooted in the Bible. Take the principle behind *habeas corpus*. In Biblical Israel six "cities of refuge" were designated for persons fleeing blood avengers. A hunted man could enter a city of refuge and demand a preliminary hearing before local elders. If they felt his case was worthy of a trial, he was given protection until a verdict was reached. From this came *habeas corpus* (Latin for "you have the body") which protects a citizen against illegal detention or imprisonment.

Our national and state constitutions are basically covenants between the people. "We the people of the United States" harks back to the Mayflower Compact, which began, "We whose names are underwritten." The Pilgrim Compact comes, through Calvin, from God's covenant promise to Israel: "Now if you obey me fully and keep my covenant, then out of all nations you will be my treasured possession."(Exodus 19:5)

It is no accident of history that the first chief justice of the U.S. Supreme Court, John Jay, was a devout Christian. This "court of last resort" is charged with determining what the law is according to the Constitution. Until recent times justices sought to discern only the intent of the writers of the Constitution in relation to a particular case: let the ruling fit the Constitution. Some justices have now changed this order: let the ruling fit the changes in society as the justices see it.

This liberal "elastic" approach has brought some terrible judgments. The Court majority decide what they think society wants or needs. Roe v. Wade, the legalization of abortion on demand, falls into this category. Courts have even imposed taxes upon people without their consent. For example, U.S. District Judge Russell G. Clark doubled school taxes in Kansas City to pay for the nation's most expensive desegregation plan. This decision was appealed by the State of Missouri to the U.S. Supreme Court which ruled that the judge could order local officials to assess the taxes.

In other words, the law becomes what the Court says it is. So what was once wrong becomes right and vice versa.

The Secularization of America

Since the early 1960's, when Bible reading and prayer in public schools were declared unconstitutional, the courts, under pressure from secular extremists, have been moving to ban Christian symbols and activities from the public arena. Never mind that these activities have been okay since America became an independent nation.

Rulings against the faith on which America was founded

have been carried to ridiculous, almost blasphemous extremes. The legal and judicial systems have so deteriorated that many public officials and business leaders fear they will be breaking the law by publicly testifying of their faith. Does this sound unbelievable? The owner of Lotz Realty in Newport News, Virginia doesn't think so.

Lotz was the target of a complaint filed by the Jewish Anti-Defamation League with the Department of Housing and Urban Development. The League charged Lotz with discriminating against non-Christians for using the Christian symbol of a fish and the words "Jesus is Coming" in company advertising. No one had ever complained that they had been harmed by the advertising of this private company. Nevertheless, HUD ordered Lotz to remove the Christian symbol, recruit employees from majority and minority religions, and send his employees to a "sensitivity" training school in civil rights.[22]

Christianity as a religion hasn't yet been declared illegal, as it was in the Roman Empire during the time of the apostles. But case by case, our freedom for public expression of faith is being whittled away.

Why is this happening? The simplest answer is that we Christians are defaulting on our obligations to be "salt" and "light" in society. The plain, sad truth is that many of us have simply removed ourselves from the system and let secularists take control of the public arena and shape society to their own perverted desires.

Nowhere is this more true than in the media, the arts, and the world of entertainment. This is the subject of the next chapter. But please don't stop there. The action section of this book follows in which I will present step-by-step directions on how we can change America.

"[The] arts crowd is engaged in a cultural struggle to root out the old America of family, faith, and flag, and recreate society in a pagan image."
Patrick Buchanan

Chapter 4

Media Power and Art Pollution

What is the first thing millions of American do in the morning?

What do most people watch while they are ironing?

What do millions of children do first when they arrive home from school?

What is the most popular evening "recreation" for most American families?

The answer to each question is the same: Watch television. This is the media age and Americans are a media people. Almost all of our information and entertainment is received from the mass media, with most coming from television. Much of what we talk about is what we hear/read/see in the mass media. And much, if not most, of our behavior is influenced by the perceptions of the world received from film, TV, videos, music, radio, newspapers, books, magazines, and other media. It is no exaggeration to say that the media has become the most powerful teaching institution in America, ahead of the family, the church, and the school.

Why Is the Media So Powerful?

The media is omnipresent, ubiquitous, and almost everywhere.

The media's message is consistent. Television, movies, novels, magazines, etc. all parrot the same secular, anti-Christian behavior. The media keeps telling us, for example, that:

- It's okay to live together before marriage.
- Abortion rights come before an unborn child's right to life.
- Gay is okay. Any type of sex is okay between consenting adults.
- If it feels right, do it. Whatever turns you on.
- Violence is the best way to settle a dispute. A typical 14-year-old child has watched the destruction of 13,000 human beings during the past five years. An average 18 year old has witnessed 15,000 murders. Twenty violent acts per hour occur on daytime children's programs.
- Church may have been okay for past generations, but it's only for the superstitious and ignorant today.
- Everybody lies.
- Patriotism is old-fashioned.

The cumulation and consonance of such media messages about sexual behavior, violence, brutality, etc. has desensitized and raised our toleration level. How would you have reacted 20 years ago if you had walked into your house and seen your children watching what almost everybody sees on TV today?

Here's how the mass media impacts our lives:

- The media sets the agenda. The media tells us what it thinks we should know.
- The media slants the issues. Makes one event or idea seem more important than others by giving it more time, space, and emphasis. The media play down, shows in a bad light, or even ignore the moral or religious side of an issue. In the last Presidential election, religious believers were depicted as rigid and not in tune with the heartbeat of mainstream America. During the 1987 visit by the Pope the TV media played up the Pope's homilies against disgruntled Catholics, homosexuals, and former priests.
- The media emphasizes negative social values more than positive ones. News tends to be negative. TV news, observes columnist James Reston, tends to sug-

gest that "everything is going wrong in our society."
- The media introduces and glamorizes new ideas, issues, fashions, immoralities, and terminology. The media has been especially successful in introducing non-Christian ideas about sex. Sex outside of marriage has, in the words of Dr. Neil Postman of New York University, been "transformed [on TV] from a dark and profound adult mystery to a product that is available to everyone like a mouthwash and underarm deodorant."[23]

The Homosexual "Slant" in Media

A few years ago the TV networks began pushing homosexuality as an acceptable, alternative life style. Here are a few examples of how they did it:

- CBS aired "Senior Trip," a movie depicting homosexuality as "normal."
- ABC "20/20" featured an interview by Barbara Walters with Harvey Fierstein, a well known homosexual. Walters made his homosexuality appear good and wholesome.
- NBC's "Hill Street Blues" showed a "good cop" being "crucified" by the public for his homosexuality.

The media changes words and images to meet ideological purposes. "Spouse" is out and "partner" in for articles/programs about male-female sexual relationships. Teenagers are "sexually active," never promiscuous. The unborn child is a mere "fetus," not a baby. Having an abortion is a part of "reproductive freedom." A pregnancy is "terminated" or a womb "emptied". A "baby" is never killed by abortion.

Unfairness in Media

News media claim to give both sides. However, media mogul Ted Turner admitted that a one hour discussion on abortion on his Cable News Network was not fair to pro-lifers. After protests arose, Turner said, "We'll give the other bozos a chance to talk back [on a program to follow]."[24]

Crowd estimates of pro-life rallies have not been reported fairly. The secular media reported only 200,000 attending the pro-life rally in Washington in April, 1990, when actually over 500,000 were there.

Why the Secular Media Doesn't Report the "God Factor" Behind Events

Quite often the secular news media misses the "God factor" in a story. Take the confession by burglar James McCord which grabbed national attention, making Watergate a national scandal.

McCord and six other defendants were being pressured not to disclose the involvement of higher-ups in the break-in to obtain information from a political office.While his trial was in progress, a troubled McCord and his wife—both church dropouts—began attending Fourth Presbyterian Church in a Washington D.C. suburb. There they heard a series of sermons by Pastor Richard Halverson on the lordship of Christ over history. Halverson said, in effect, that every person has a bent toward evil, to be his own god, to set up standards and plans apart from God. When leaders do this, the results are compounded, and as one rises in leadership the peril increases. Because of our rejection of God, we experience frustration and a sense of futility.

How we handle our problems, McCord heard Halverson say, becomes the crucial question. The Christian knows that God will ultimately triumph, and in the meantime is working out everything for good in the lives of those who love Him. Only as we place complete trust in Christ can we experience real freedom and release from tension amid the tribulations of life.

During the trial—while McCord and his wife continued to attend church—the defendants remained under pressure not to disclose the involvement of their bosses in the break-in.

On the Sunday after being found guilty, McCord returned home from church wrestling with a decision. Without asking his lawyer, he drafted and delivered a letter to Judge John Sirica, telling the judge that higher-ups involved in the break-in had gone unnamed. The letter, when disclosed to the press, made Watergate a national event. But no one in the secular media managed to discover McCord's motivation for making the disclosure. McCord says he did it as a result of Halverson's sermons and to get his spiritual and moral house in order.[25]

Such an oversight isn't surprising. The secular media tends to be deaf and dumb to religious influences in the shape of events. This helps explain why the national sports media is virtually silent about the Christian activities of some national sports figures. Most of the national baseball and football teams have "prayer chapels," but you'd never know that from the sports commentators who also tend to keep quiet about religious actions on the field. Example: In a recent close National Football League game, a Philadelphia Eagles player ran for a touchdown against the Denver Broncos. When the player crossed the goal line, he immediately knelt in prayer for about 10 seconds. The picture made this obvious, yet the commentators made no mention of the incident.

The Media Is Out to Reshape Society

The now famous Lichter-Rothman survey of media influentials found two thirds of the leaders in television and films agreeing that TV and film should be used to reshape society. When asked which institutions have the most influence in society, the majority put religion next to last, just above the military.

Said Lee Rich, an influential film producer: "The church has been narrow minded. It hasn't grown with the times. It's been lumbering along and hasn't taken cognizance of what's going on in the world. It hasn't made the changes it's got to make. The church brought us up to believe that things were the way they made them out to be. As we've become wiser and more educated, we've started to challenge these implanted beliefs." Rich added that he hadn't "been to church in 40 years and I don't know a single person who does go to church."[26]

The Anti-Christ Element in the Media

In most movies and in TV dramas, Christianity goes
unmentioned or is subtly presented in a negative way.
Rock star Lisa Hartman, for example, was shown having
a steamy affair with TV evangelist Joshua Reynolds, who
happened to be a virgin when he met her. The TV movie
"Celebrity" featured a TV evangelist named Thomas
Jeremiah Luther, who was a con man, liar, cheat, and a
rapist.

Some shocking examples of anti-religious commercial
movies:

- The film "Monsignor" stars Christopher Reeves (the
  "Superman" actor) as a corrupt priest who seduces
  an idealistic nun and does business with the Mafia.
- "The Blob" stars a small-town pastor who turns out
  to be a secret alcoholic. The final scene shows him
  threatening the end of the world.
- "Poltergeist II" features a hymn-singing preacher as
  the villain who leads a band of fanatic Bible-belters
  trying to drag a worldly suburban family down to
  hell.
- "King David" stars Richard Gere in the role of the
  Jewish King David who abandons his religious
  "delusions" and rejects God at the end of his life.
- "The Last Temptation of Christ" depicts Jesus as
  having brain fever, being shocked by his magical
  powers, and lusting for Mary Magdalene. In one
  scene Jesus is shown waiting in line at Mary
  Magadalene's brothel, then entering a darkened
  room where she lies naked.
- "The Handmaid's Tale," now ready for the theaters,
  portrays life in the Nazi-like nation of Gilead, whose
  constitution is the Old Testament and whose leaders
  coerce fertile young women into bearing their
  children, while uncooperative women work in toxic
  dumps where they die within a year. The pro-abortion movement plans to use this despicable film—
  which Playboy praises for its "cool eroticism,
  intelligence, and intensity"—in fund raising.[27]

Yes, there is an occasional movie of merit. Award-winning "Driving Miss Daisy" portrays a rich and honorable friendship between a black chauffeur and a Southern Jewish woman of culture and wealth. "Tender Mercies" is about a sweet and devoutly religious elderly woman who seeks to revisit her childhood home in Texas once more before she dies. "A Cry in the Dark" won an Oscar for dramatizing the true story of an Australian minister's wife falsely accused of killing her baby.

Such films are commendable, but about as rare as finding a four-leaf clover in a shopping center parking lot.

I haven't even talked about soap operas which offer lessons in seduction and adultery.

The scene in art and literature is no better. Have you read recent reviews of the latest books on which many movies made for theaters and TV are based?

A book by Scribner, for example, "shows us how a man's damaged mind works, before and after he's surprised by his own crime"[28]

What Lisa Knew: The Truths and Lies of the Steinberg Case "paints a horrifying picture of a sadomasochistic relationship."[29]

These are typical of what you see in bookstores today. However, the problems didn't originate there, but with publishers and writers who hold nothing sacred anymore.[30]

How Our Tax Money Supports Obscene "Art"

Anyone for taxpayer-subsidized art? I mentioned a few examples in an earlier chapter. Here are some more that may make you throw up on your living room rug. The Federal National Endowment for the Arts dished out $65,000 for the Gay Sunshine Press and the Panjandrum Press to publish explicit homosexual stories. The San Francisco lesbian and gay film festival got $10,000 in 1989 and expects $20,000 in 1990. Ten thousand dollars helped pay for a New York art exhibit which denounced Cardinal John J. O'Connor as a fat cannibal and a black-skirted creep.

This is not all. We taxpayers helped pay for a New York art exhibit that was advertised with drawings of Senator Jesse Helms nailed to a cross. This exhibit also encouraged

viewers to walk on an American flag. Tax money also
provided $15,000 to the University Galleries at Illinois
State University to help fund a "Tongues of Flame" exhibit
which showed Christ injecting drugs into his arm, with a
needle and a syringe, the Christ child wielding a pistol,
and other sexually perverted scenes.

Perversion in Music

Have you watched the latest rock videos, which your
children can rent for two or three dollars from almost any
video store? Got a strong stomach? Watch MTV for an hour
sometime. You'll find music that pushes drugs, perver-
sions of all kinds, suicide and rebellion against family and
society.

Are you a country music fan? If so, you know about the
dirty lyrics in some songs which are sung to family audien-
ces at the Grand Ole Opry and county fairs.

Where Have All the Moral Standards Gone?

What's gone wrong with our news and entertainment,
music, art, and literature?

The answer is simple. Standards no longer exist. There
is no moral consensus on what makes a good book or movie.
The truth of God is changed into a lie. Uncleanness reigns
as the "beautiful people"—the models set forth for our
children—dishonor their own bodies in sordid relationships and animal-like intimacies.

As in the days of the Hebrew judges, "every man [does]
that which is right in his own eyes." (Judges 17:6)

That's what is happening in American society today. We
are in a time of moral anarchy, not unlike that which
preceded the fall of the once mighty Roman Empire to the
pagan hordes of Europe.

That is the bad news which we must face.

The good news is that many of us are awakening to the
danger that imperils our nation and the future of our
children. With God's help, we are determined to change
America.

"The men who succeed best in public life are those who take the risk of standing by their convictions."
James A. Garfield

Chapter 5

You're not Alone

". . . I am the only one left; and now they are trying to kill me too."(I Kings 19:10)

We've all felt as the prophet Elijah did when oppressed by evil. Yet the Lord assured him that "seven thousand in Israel . . . have not bowed down to Baal." (I Kings 19:18)

There have always been faithful servants of God and righteousness—action people who see a job to be done and do it.

- Fabiola saw people dying on the streets of Rome from lack of medical care. She went to work and opened the first charity hospital of record in A.D. 380.
- Thalasius was haunted by hordes of blind beggars who had no place to go. He opened the first home for the blind.
- Dorothea Dix, a frail, sickly American Sunday school teacher in the last century, discovered "crazy" people were being kept in prison dungeons. By speaking to legislatures and rallies of concerned citizens, she influenced the building of hospitals for the mentally ill in the U.S., Canada, and Europe.
- Anthony Ashley Cooper, known as Lord Shaftesbury, found children as young as seven working in factories from before dawn until late at night and given only a cot and starvation meals. He persuaded the British Parliament to pass laws that outlawed such cruelty. Lord Shaftesbury said, "A Christian

has a moral obligation to provide for the spiritual, physical, and social needs of the less fortunate."[31]

- William Wilberforce decided to do something about slavery. He was responsible for getting laws passed that outlawed this monstrous evil in England.
- Harriet Beecher Stowe set out to do something about slavery in America. She wrote the book Uncle Tom's Cabin, which convinced millions of Americans that the black slaves in America must be set free.

These and many other Christian activists didn't sit around wishing that the government, the Chamber of Commerce, or some big corporation with influence and power "would do something about THAT." They saw a need and did something about it.

Not incidentally, one of the best kept secrets in America is that almost all of the great social reforms which we now take for granted were initiated by devout Christians.

If the media would take its secular blinders off, it might discover that Christians continue to be at the forefront of helping change America for the better today.

Here are some modern Christians who have done something:

Charles Colson of Watergate Fame

When Charles Colson was sentenced to a one to three-year prison term, Colson told the judge, "I have committed my life to Jesus Christ. I can work for the Lord in prison or out of prison, and that's how I want to spend my life."[32]

While in prison, Colson found a skilled doctor, imprisoned for a non-violent crime, running the washing machine. Says Colson: He "could have been made to work giving free medical help to the poor, contributing to the community rather than costing it about $15,000 a year to keep him in prison. But there he was, stirring suds."

As Colson observed this man and other non-violent prisoners, he concluded that "the system . . . wasn't doing anything to restore or rehabilitate [prisoners]; it was just warehousing them. It's not hard to understand why 74 percent of released prisoners are rearrested within four years."

Colson didn't just observe and complain. He started Prison Fellowship. Thousands of men and women are now out of jail and leaving productive lives because of Colson's work. Colson, who terms himself "a law and order conservative," has called for Christians to join him and other Prison Fellowship workers in improving the criminal justice system.[33]

Mel and Norma Gabler, Textbook Analysts

In the friendly community of Hawkins, Texas, the Gablers were regarded as community pillars. Both were active in a Baptist church where Mel was a deacon and Norma superintendent of the youth department. Mel, a pipeline clerk who had only a year in college, and Norma, just a high school graduate, wanted to do everything they could to help their three sons get a good education. This included backing up the local teachers and getting involved in PTA. What they didn't know was how involved they would become.

One day after school their teenage son, Jim asked Mel a history question: "What was the intent of our founding fathers when they wrote the Constitution?"

Mel replied, "They intended to establish a government which would be strong enough to unite the American people, but which would leave them as much of their God-given freedom as possible, with most of the governing left up to state and local governments."

Jim held up his text and grimaced. "Not according to my textbook, Dad."

As Mel looked on in puzzlement, Jim showed him where the book listed the powers granted the Federal Government and limitations on the states. "There is nothing in this book, Dad, about the rights and freedoms retained by the people and the states."[34]

Mel and Norma began looking into other history texts. They found many familiar stories missing. Nathan Hale's "I only regret I have but one life to lose for my country" was absent from most books. So was Patrick Henry's "Give me liberty or give me death." And there was only a brief sentence in one book about the loyalty of George Washington's army at Valley Forge and nothing about his deep religious faith.

How were the new textbooks selected? School officials told the Gablers that Texas law required the local district to select from a state-approved list drawn up by the State Textbook Committee, appointed by the State Board of Education.

The Gablers gathered information from other concerned parents. They sent information on objectionable books to their Christmas card list. They telephoned a popular radio call-in host. After hearing the Gablers' comments by phone, the host invited Mel and Norma to come to the studio and answer questions for an hour-and-a-half.

The Gablers soon discovered that other parents had already been complaining that the new books tended to be anti-American, giving short shrift to patriotism, morality, free enterprise, individual and states' rights, while promoting federal programs, secular humanism, dirty literature (disguised as "social realism"), and many left-wing ideas.

Norma and son Jim went to the state capital and testified before a legislative committee investigating un-Americanism in textbooks. When Norma spoke she was booed by some spectators and treated discourteously by members of the committee. But when Jim spoke the room became strangely quiet. Among other things he noted his history text left the "impression that George Washington did little more than . . . Benedict Arnold" in winning American independence

The Gablers carried their fight to the State Board of Education and the general public. Publishers were forced to change and rewrite scores of textbooks, in order to sell their books to Texas schools. Mel and Norma were particularly successful in persuading publishers to include more about America's religious heritage.

Norma testified scores of times before the state school board, textbook adoption committees, and in other public hearings on textbooks. In one instance a lawyer board member challenged her to "tell what qualifies you for us to listen to anything you have to say."

Norma looked him squarely in the eye. "Yes, sir, I have three qualifications. First, I am a mother of three sons.

Second, I am a taxpayer whose money pays for these books. Third, I am a registered voter, who by law you represent. Can you think of three better reasons?"

The lawyer could not and said, "Go ahead, Mrs. Gabler."[35]

Norma did and during the next two decades she and Mel became the two most influential parents in textbook adoption in America. They appeared on "Donahue" three times and on "Sixty Minutes," "Today," "Good Morning America," and many other broadcasts.

Edward Jenkinson, a leading opponent of the Gablers, admitted on "60 Minutes": "They probably have more influence on the use of textbooks in this country than any other two people. . . . I don't think that two people should have that power. . . . I think that a teacher must have the right to teach so that students will have the right to know, and I believe that those two rights are guaranteed by the First Amendment."

Replied Norma Gabler on the same program: "Now, it's strange that if they choose it, it's academic freedom; it's a right of selection. But, if we do it, it's censorship. The highest form of censorship is denying a parent's right to be heard, and who is doing that? The professionals. I call that censorship. And if you [parents] don't fight, nobody else will."[36]

Beverly LaHaye, Concerned Women for America

My friend Bev LaHaye's moment of realization came when she attended a women's conference and heard Betty Friedan, founder of the National Organization for Women. A pastor's wife for over 25 years, Beverly LaHaye had given her energies to her husband, Tim, and their church. She became alarmed when hearing Betty Friedan's claim to be the voice of all women. "She doesn't speak for me," Beverly told herself.

She called together nine other concerned Christian women to discuss how they might stop the so-called Equal Rights Amendment. After 60 meetings and a successful pro-American rally, Beverly founded Concerned Women for America to protect the family through prayer action. Since CWA's conception, it has grown to be the largest women's organization in America with chapters in all 50 states. In my state of Wisconsin alone, there are 1,847 members and we're still growing.

Through speaking and in the CWA monthly magazine, Beverly keeps members informed on current issues, prayer requests, how they can get involved through registering people to vote, calling and writing their elected representatives, opposing specific bills that affect the family, and writing effective letters.

Concerned Women for America also aids Christians who suffer persecution for standing by their convictions. Take John Larson of Fresno, CA who quit his job at a drug store because the store sold alcohol and lottery tickets which he felt violated his Christian beliefs. Because of this he was denied unemployment benefits by the state. A CWA attorney informed state officials that the U.S. Supreme Court had ruled four times that a person cannot be denied compensation for losing his job because of religious convictions. [37]

Beverly's husband Tim served as a pastor of a large church in San Diego for 25 years where he started a Christian high school and a college, before resigning to enter a larger public ministry. The LaHayes now live in Washington D.C. where Tim directs Family Life Seminars and Beverly leads Concerned Women of America. This dynamic couple now have a powerful influence through their books, seminars, and rallies for the preservation of traditional values.

John W. Whitehead: A Lawyer for America's Heritage

One of the leading constitutional attorneys in the United States, John Whitehead founded the Rutherford Institute, a national legal/educational organization that deals in lawsuits relating to free speech and free exercise of religion.

Says Whitehead: "Historically, the freedom to live and work out one's religious beliefs, without fear of government interference, has made the United States a haven from religious oppression. But the situation is changing rapidly. America is secularizing at a breakneck pace. Increasingly, forces hostile to the effects of religion in society are challenging the right to express a belief in God in the public arena."[38]

Whitehead and his law associates in the Rutherford Institute have served as legal counsel to many individual Christians, churches, and Christian organizations who have been taken to court for exercising their religious liberty rights. They came to the aid of Christian parents in Greenville, TN who objected to their children being forced to read school texts containing materials disparaging to their faith. A lower federal court ruled for the parents, but was overruled by a federal appeals court arguing that the parents did not have the right to isolate their children from objectionable ideas in public schools.

Whitehead, who has authored 12 books, encourages Christians to organize strong parent concern groups for involvement in community affairs and watch over areas that affect the family. But he emphasizes that this is not enough. "Parents must become more active with their children. My wife and I read to our children nightly, and not just Christian magazines, but also such periodicals as Smithsonian and Newsweek. We want our kids to know what the larger world is thinking."[39]

Don Wildmon: Fighter Against Mind Pollutants

Christmas, 1976. Picture a Mississippi Methodist minister and his family gathered around the TV in their den, thinking that they "might laugh together or that we might all hold our breath in suspense . . . . Instead, our three choices on the prime-time television menu were promiscuous sex, crude profanity, and gratuitous violence."[40]

Don Wildmon became angry as he reflected on the deterioration of television. He did some research and found that children entering kindergarten that year could expect to witness 13,000 TV killings by the time they entered high school. He suspected that sexual immorality was also a big problem, and it was. He found that the PTA and some national public figures were beginning to speak out against gratuitous sex and violence, but nobody had organized with specific goals in mind.

Wildmon went to work, starting his battle to clean up TV and pornography with only a secondhand desk in his living room. He asked other concerned citizens to join him for a "Turn-The-TV-Off Week" in early 1977. He sent releases to area news media. The Associated Press picked up the story. Fifteen hundred letters of support poured into his church.

In 1978 Wildmon could hardly believe his eyes when he read in a Memphis newspaper that CBS-TV had purchased the rights to Pete Hamill's novel about a woman having a "a love affair with her tough boxer son. . . ." "I made a major decision," Wildmon recalls. "The time had come, [for me] to take a stand . . . to draw the line and say, Enough is enough! I had to try and stop CBS from exploitatively airing yet another form of perverted sex." Wildmon wrote 250 TV sponsors informing them of a proposed boycott if they advertised on the show and he asked supporters and friends to write letters of protest to CBS-TV president James Rosenfield.

Although Wildmon's efforts resulted in only a postponement and a slight rewrite of the incestuous movie, it became the most protested program in the history of network TV. Many companies refused to advertise resulting in the network losing more than four million dollars in revenues. More than that, CBS learned that thousands upon thousands of Americans were no longer going to remain quiet about TV perversion and trash.[41]

Wildmon next formed The National Federation for Decency, now known as the American Family Association. At first he simply urged people to call or write the networks and protest the worst programs. Network officials replied politely that they would never "surrender those durable moral values that give our nation its spiritual foundation," as one stated. Nothing changed until Wildmon organized picketing and boycotting of large chain stores. Sears withdrew their ads from two big TV shows and 7-Eleven pulled pornographic magazines from company stores.

In 1981 Wildmon spoke to the National Broadcasters Association for Community Affairs and cited several examples of discrimination against religion. The audience turned hostile as hisses and even profanity were hurled at him. Wildmon became known as "the man the networks love to hate."

In 1988 Wildmon led a boycott against the blasphemous film, "The Last Temptation of Christ." This time scores of national church leaders joined him in a coalition. Hundreds of theaters refused to show the film.

Building on the momentum, Wildmon and his partners lined up an even broader coalition of church leaders for "Christian Leaders for Responsible Television (CLeaR TV). They warned advertisers of their plan to research all TV to find the worst all-round sponsor. That company was then boycotted by Christians nationwide for an entire year. In July, 1989, they announced that the Mennen and Clorox companies had tied for the dubious award. This boycott is now in progress.[42]

"Advertising on network TV in prime time costs $300,000 a minute," Wildmon notes. "If advertisers who respect the family and the Christian community pull out of offensive programming, each network will lose one ad minute per night, and I believe that's a conservative estimate. That's a $9-million loss in one month. If they lose two minutes a night, they'll lose $19 million a month. If they lose that much, we expect they will begin to change their programming."[43]

Dr. James Dobson: Focus on the Family

When President Jimmy Carter announced a White House Conference on the Family, 80,000 people wrote to ask that Dr. James Dobson be a panelist. After hearing Dobson in one session, James Guy Tucker, the chairman of the conference, said, "I did not know until recently that people . . . . with university credentials believed the kinds of things that you believe."[44]

Christian broadcaster and publisher James Dobson went on to become the most influential spokesman for traditional family values in America. His organization, Focus on the Family, with over 500 employees, receives from 30-40,000 letters each week. Fifty million people have reportedly seen his eight-part family film series. Politicians tremble at the number of letters he can generate on a family issue. When government officials demoted Health and Human Services official Joanne

Gasper for her anti-abortion decisions, Dobson inspired the sending of 100,000 letters of protest to the White House. The pro-life official was given back her power.

Dobson, the only son of a Nazarene preacher, decided to become a psychologist after an interview with Dr. Clyde Narramore. In straightforward fashion he earned a Ph.D., accepted a position at Children's Hospital of Los Angeles, and was appointed as a professor of pediatrics at the University of Southern California Medical School. At Children's Hospital he oversaw one of the most important studies ever made on mental retardation.

Living near Hollywood, Dr. Dobson became aware that traditional family values were coming under attack in films. He began conducting seminars. His first book, <u>Dare to Discipline</u>, became a bestseller. When invitations to speak began pouring in, he decided that his own family was more important than traveling to distant places. He stopped the seminars and made a video series on family concerns. That year, 1977, he and a group of associates established Focus on the Family. His publisher, Tyndale, provided a $40,000 grant which enabled him to begin the broadcast that is now heard on over 1100 stations.

Dobson doesn't see himself as a broadcast evangelist. His personal integrity is unassailable. He takes no salary from Focus on the Family and pays the organization a monthly sum for book royalties believed to result from publicity on the broadcast. His main concern is the family, beginning with his wife Shirley and his children. His message is that family life is a noble and godly calling. He never becomes involved in political campaigns or preaches on foreign relations. "But I assure you," he declares, "that we will fight to the death for the moral values in which we believe."

James Dobson fears for the future of America. "If the [humanistic change agents] are successful," he warns, "your grandchildren will grow up in a godless nation that has no personal memory of our faith. . . . The most important struggle by far is the contest for the right to control the minds of the next generation. Those who decide what children see, hear, think, and believe will ultimately shape the future of the nation." [45]

Pat Robertson: Christian Broadcaster

Pat Robertson is the son of a prominent U.S. senator and descendant of two U.S. presidents from his mother's family tree. After graduating from Yale Law School, failing his bar exam, and becoming bored in his business, Pat decided to go into the ministry because "I just have a feeling I can do something good for mankind."

His mother asked, "How can you go into the ministry until you know Jesus Christ?" A week later a Dutchman named Cornelius Vanderbreggen told Pat what it really meant to be a Christian. Pat went home and told his wife, Dede, about his personal relationship with Christ. She thought he merely meant that they would be going to church more regularly. When Pat started uncapping liquor bottles and pouring the contents down the drain, she knew it was "pretty serious." When he gave up cigars and foul language, she knew something had definitely happened to her husband. That was in 1956.

Only a nominal church-goer, Dede became hysterical when Pat sold all their possessions, gave the money to charity, and moved his young family to the Brooklyn slums to identify with the poor. Fortunately, Dede recovered, became a Christian at a Bible camp, and backed Pat while he went to seminary and served as associate pastor of a church.

Instead of settling into a pastorate, Pat decided God wanted him to buy a closed, vandalized TV station in a rundown building on a dead end street in Portsmouth, VA. That he had only $70 didn't keep him from asking the owner, a used car dealer, to give him a six month option to buy the station for $37,000. To Pat's amazement the owner agreed.

Pat now had to raise the money for the purchase and repair of the station. He opened a bank account with $3. With the cost of a checkbook subtracted, the account was $3 overdrawn. He had business cards printed with the call letters WTFC-TV Television for Christ. On the back he printed a list of prayer requests: 1. Wisdom to know how to buy a station. 2. God's blessing in the negotiations to buy it. 3. Favor with the Federal Communications Commission. 4. A nationwide broadcast ministry.

To support his family he took a temporary job as minister of education for a Portsmouth church at $100 a week. Contributions began trickling in, but there was not enough to complete the purchase. The owner finally decided to simply deed over the property with the condition that Pat pay the station's debts.

On October 1, 1961, after spending all night getting equipment ready, Pat spoke into a microphone: "My name is Pat Robertson. Welcome to the Christian Broadcasting Network."

The vision enlarged. The annual budget increased to $120,000. The daily "700 Club" went on the air. A year later CBN was carried by cable systems in over 4,000 communities. By 1978 the network had a staff of over 700 and had outlets in Latin America, Africa, and Asia.

Pat envisioned an International Communications Center and a major university. In 1979 CBN's new headquarters was dedicated in Virginia Beach, VA. Billy Graham gave the keynote address.

By 1985 the Nielsen rating service was estimating that 4.4 million people in the U.S. were watching the 700 Club every day and 27 million Americans were viewing at least a portion of the program each month. Almost every day Pat hosted the "700 Club," welcoming U.S. cabinet members, congressmen, psychiatrists, ex-KGB men, sociologists, and other guests. He talked about the morality of government budget deficits, relationships with the Soviet Union, welfare, abortion, prayer in schools, and many other provocative subjects. Pat never hesitated to voice his opinion.

"For the sake of our children," Pat said, "we must bring God back to the classroom. Ninety-four percent of all Americans believe in God. Only six percent are atheists. I do not believe that the 94 percent of us who believe in God have any duty whatsoever to dismantle our entire public affirmation of faith in God."[46]

The university which Pat Robertson founded is now open with graduate schools of communication, education, business, Biblical studies, and public policy, plus a law school bequeathed by Oral Roberts University. The university is an integral part of Pat's vision to do all he can to change America.

In 1986 Pat announced his candidacy for president of the United States. He was largely ignored by many media until he defeated both George Bush and Jack Kemp in Michigan's selection of delegates to the Republican National Convention. Pat now became a national figure in the secular press, under such headlines as "Pat Robertson Seeks a Lower Office," "The Wacko Factor," and "Heaven Only Knows." Many, however, accepted Pat as a serious candidate. Sociologist Jeffrey Hadden declared, "Pat really sees God moving in history with a plan and America as His chosen land for its fulfillment."[47]

I was one of hundreds of thousands of people who worked for Pat. I served as his state campaign manager for Wisconsin. Naturally we were disappointed when he didn't win the nomination. Pat, however, refused to quit. He went back to CBN and to the 700 Club and the university where he continues to do his bit to change America for God and for good.

A Teacher in Missouri Acts Against Indecency

I could mention many other nation changers. Some have national influence. Others, like Sally Tierney, are not so well known.

Sally's moment of decision came one morning when she was driving to Fox Junior High School in Arnold, MO where she was a teacher and assistant principal. She recalls, "I had the radio on in my car. . . at a time when a lot of kids listen to the radio on the way to school. . .when I heard a disc jockey reading a graphic description of oral sex." The DJ was reading excerpts from a Playboy magazine interview with Jessica Hahn in which she described having sex with TV evangelist Jim Bakker.

She sent a complaint to the Federal Communications Commission in Washington. On October 26, 1989, the FCC, under its new chairman, former Missouri broadcaster Alfred C. Sikes, took action against KSD-FM in St. Louis, and on a number of other allegations of indecency on the radio airways. This was a direct result of petitions by Sally Tierney and other concerned citizens. The FCC gave KSD-FM and several other radio stations 30 days to respond formally to complaints of indecent broadcasts. The FCC cited a federal law stating: "Whoever utters any obscene, indecent, or profane language by means of radio communication shall be fined not more than $10,000 or imprisoned not more than two years or both." The Commission noted a federal court decision defining indecent material as "language or material that, in context, depicts or describes, in terms patently offensive as measured by contemporary community standards for the broadcast medium, sexual, or excretory activities or organs."

The American Civil Liberties Union objected. "When the government gets into regulating what you can—or can't—hear on the radio, then we're on a slippery slope," warned Colleen O'Connor, a spokeswoman for the organization.[48] But the ACLU and other left-wing organizations who seem to see no limits on what is allowable in the public media will not have their way so long as citizens like Sally Tierney are taking action and alerting the government agency which licenses stations.

The Price Maria Paid

Maria Hernandez and her husband Carlos made repeated reports to the police about drug dealing in front of their house in Brooklyn, NY. Everybody in the neighborhood knew about the drug dealers, but only Maria and Carlos were brave enough to protest. They kept going to the police even after Carlos was shot and stabbed.

A few mornings later Maria was shot through her window as she was dressing for work. Carlos, still suffering from his wounds, walked beside Maria's coffin in a three-mile procession of mourners to the cemetery. The mayor and several other officials joined the walk, but it was Maria and Carlos' action, when reported across the country, that inspired hundreds of other citizens to rise up and take action against the merchants of death.

Residents in many cities are now marching to show their opposition to drug trafficking. In the eighth police district of St. Louis, for example, citizen protesters gathered on the parking lot of the Hopewell Baptist Church and marched through the neighborhood demanding that drug dealers leave. City official Virvus Jones, who took part in this protest, suggested residents "picket the crack houses and make it uncomfortable" for them until they were either arrested or left the neighborhood.

Going Back to School

Many who decided to do something discovered they needed to go back to school. Illinois mother Pat Likes took in a foster child with dyslexia. The teacher refused to listen to Pat's opinion about the boy's problem and snapped, "Don't come back and bother me again until you're qualified to speak on this subject."

The teacher's challenge moved Pat to return to school and finish college. She developed her writing skills and co-authored two books on children with special problems from a Christian perspective.[49]

I could fill the rest of this book with more examples of individuals who refused to sit idly by while America goes down the drain. You never know what can be accomplished until you decide to do something. When you do, you'll discover that many, many other people share the same concern.

Take a Lesson from the Gablers

If you really intend to get involved, you must start by doing your homework. Otherwise, you're likely to fail, become discouraged, and quit.

For example, if you want to get better textbooks into public schools, consider these tips from Mel and Norma Gabler.

- Know the legal rights you have in regard to your child's education. The Federal Protection of Pupil Rights law, better known as the "Hatch Act," forbids schools to (1) subject students to psychological examination or treatment, (2) require students to reveal "political affiliations," or (3) ask students to make "critical appraisals" of behavior and attitudes of family members without the "prior written consent of the parent."

- Act before your school purchases the offensive books. Typically, a parent becomes upset about a single book that has already been approved and slotted into school curriculum. It is then usually too late to do much more than create a community fuss in which you might get only one book removed. It's much better to "shoot" for major changes in curriculum that will benefit education in your area for years to come.
- Secure review copies of books which will be "up" for adoption for the coming year. In Texas, publishers are required to place these books in regional educational libraries. Even if you must buy the books from the publishers, review them before the local textbook adoption committee meets.
- Be selective in what you review. Take one subject of concern each year. Good reviews of many textbooks are available by writing the Gablers at P.O. Box 7518, Longview, TX 75601.
- Develop friendly relations with your local school board, school officials, and your child's teachers.
- Build a parents' group. Show objectionable material to key business and civic leaders. Try to get influential persons on your side before you speak at any public meeting.
- Write your state education office for information on procedures for textbook adoption and how parents can be involved. Oklahoma, Texas, and several other states require curriculum to be objective, teach high moral standards, promote the work ethic, teach the principles and benefits of free enterprise, and emphasize traditional family roles.
- Be well prepared for press interviews. When speaking to groups, know ahead of time what you will say. Anticipate counter-arguments and objections in public meetings.
- Simplify the semantics. Explain such terms as "values clarification" when necessary. Ask educators to define "educationese" that they may use.
- Stick to issues. Keep your cool. Avoid personalties.
- Always leave your opponent an "out." He may say he

doesn't agree with the book, but is only following orders.

- Hold some of your best points back, just in case you need to make a comeback.
- Keep on the offensive. You and your beliefs are not on trial. Offensive textbooks are.
- Above all, pray for guidance for yourself and the people you are addressing.[50] Mel and Norma Gabler, Charles Colson, Beverly LaHaye, Don Wildmon, Pat Robertson, John Whitehead, Dr. James Dobson, and many others have shown us the way. If you want to do something to change America, you won't have to look far to find an opportunity to join other concerned citizens. Special citizen groups are popping up all across the country to attack the problems and influences that are rapidly undermining our nation.

You are not alone. The question is: Are you willing to step through the doorway of responsibility and join others who are determined to change our country?

God bless you as you move in this direction.

"Homes are the building blocks of civilization."
Arnold Toynbee

Chapter 6

Impacting the Media

A recent study by the prestigious 39,000 member American Academy of Pediatrics found that long-term TV viewing is a major cause of violent or aggressive behavior in children and contributes substantially to childhood obesity. By the time a young American of today reaches age 70, the study predicted, he will have spent seven years watching television. The investigation found that soap operas offer the worst examples of sex on TV and are shown when small children often watch TV.[51]

Start With Yourself and Your Family

Columnist Mike Royko, who makes no claim to being an evangelical Christian, says there are two parts to the TV problem as presented by the Academy of Pediatrics.

First, says Royko, "there is the source. That would be those who run television and those who produce the movies and the other drivel shown on TV. Having dealt with movie makers and TV entertainment executives, I would rate their ethics, sense of public and professional responsibility, and business aspirations on about the same level as the average pimp."

The second part, according to Royko, "would be the parents of the kids who average three to four hours a day in front of the tube. And those who pay little or no attention to what their kids watch."[52]

Most of us cannot do much to change the source, except perhaps through boycotts of sponsor products and other protests. The Bible gives us guidelines for mind food.

Philippians 4:8 is a good place to start. It tells us to think about things that are true, pure, honest, just, lovely, of good report, virtuous, and worthy of praise.

Try selecting what you read and watch with that guideline in mind. I can guarantee that your thought life will improve and you'll have greater peace of mind. Now you're ready to start with those in your charge. We can do something about our media habits and those of our children. Here's how:

- "Discipline your media consumption," Billy Graham told the National Association of Religious Broadcasters, "We've found that the media habits of Christians are basically no different from non-Christians."[53] Is this true of your family? Are you as selective in what you read and see as in what you eat? As you think in your heart, Scripture declares, so are you. (Proverbs 23:7) And Scripture commands, "Keep your heart with all diligence; for out of it are the issues of life." (Proverbs 4:23) Deciding on what you will read and watch is a lot like making out a grocery list. You write down and buy what is needed to prepare nutritious, healthful meals. If you're on a special diet, you follow the guidelines of a tried and tested program.

- Set limits on when, what, and how much TV your children may watch. Even too much "good" TV can make a child more passive and also hurt his school work. Decide what programs and/or channels the child may not watch and, unless you have a good reason, do not watch them yourself.

- Watch TV with your children at times. Discuss with them actions and opinions of characters. Help them see what is right and wrong by your family's standards. When a non-Biblical lifestyle is presented, talk about it with your children. Show them where your values differ and why. Also, watch the nightly news with your children. Help your children learn the difference between a balanced and an unbalanced report and to recognize when the traditional moral view is unfairly presented.

- Provide alternative entertainment. Show good videos on your VCR which you can rent or buy at your local Christian bookstore. Focus on the Family's "McGee and Me" is an excellent series of network-quality programs which can be ordered. Tyndale House Publishers is another good source for Christian videos.
- Keep good books and Christian magazines in plain sight around the house. Again, your Christian book store will be helpful. An especially good four-color children's magazine is published by the Moody Bible Institute and called simply Kids.
- Play games with your children. Take them on outings. Don't let them become prisoners of TV or of any other media which may poison their minds or stunt their mental processes. The American Academy of Pediatrics recommends that parents limit children's viewing to one to two hours daily and that parents develop family activities such as reading, athletics, and hobbies.

Put the Heat on Broadcasters and Sponsors

- Convey your opinion on programs to local stations, the networks, and especially sponsors. Tell them what you like or don't like and why by sharing with them the Biblical principle behind your convictions. The American Academy of Pediatrics supports legislation making broadcast of high-quality children's programming a condition of station license renewal and mandating at least one hour per day of educational children's programs.
- Provide postal cards for your children to express their reaction, positive and negative, to certain shows. Mail the cards to sponsors.
- Participate in boycotts of the products of companies that sponsor the most offensive TV programs. Donald Wildmon's Christian Leaders for Responsible Television (CLeaR-TV) has achieved notable success with such boycotts.
- Use media technology and techniques in the education program and worship services of your church.

Tim LaHaye teaches old-fashioned, Biblical values with an overhead projector. He "believe[s] Jesus would have used an overhead, if the technology had been available in His time."

Community Action on Pornography

When you have your own house in order, it's time to begin in your community. Vickie and Hazel live in a family neighborhood of a city in southwestern Minnesota. They became alarmed over pornographic material in a drug store where their pre-school children bought fruit. Both women courteously asked the owner to place the offensive magazines out of the children's sight. The owner declined, saying, "Just keep your kids away from this part of the store." Vickie and Hazel didn't give up. They went door to door getting names on a petition, and when that didn't work they organized a march outside the store. Within two hours the magazines were put behind the counter.

Rock music and pornographic videos have become a big part of the media. Just how bad has rock music become? Some of the least offensive rock music today would have been thrown out of a tavern 20 years ago. Much of the current rock music is sick, sadistic, sacrilegious, and some is even Satanistic.

Do You Know What Your Children Are Hearing and Seeing?

Don't take my word for it. If you care at all for children, I dare you to listen to some of the records and tapes and watch some of the videos which kids can get easily today. If you have a gram of decency, your blood will boil. To call some of this stuff trash is unfair to the waste collection industry. Unfortunately, too many parents are either "too busy," don't care, or don't want to know what their kids are watching. If they really looked at some of the videos, they might get as angry and sick as Tipper Gore, the wife of Senator Albert Gore, Jr., and Susan Baker, wife of Secretary of State James A. Baker III, did when they discovered what their kids could get at the friendly local music and video stores.

Mrs. Gore, a Democrat, and Mrs. Baker, a Republican, didn't sit around stewing in their own juices. They organized the Parents' Music Resource Center to make parents aware of what their children were hearing on some rock music records and tapes. Acting under pressure from this group, the major record companies agreed to put warning labels on records that might contain controversial lyrics about sex, drugs, or violence. This and other actions resulted in a Senate Commerce Committee hearing in which Senator Albert Gore took part.

A rumor was spread that the government might censor rock and rap music, although Mrs. Gore had repeatedly said they were not protesting the right of the recording industry to make and sell such music. The entertainment industry applied such pressure that Senator Gore apologized for the hearing. Can you imagine? When the Parents' Music Resource Center continued its protests, rock and roll and rap musicians staged a counter rally across from the White House. Surprise! Surprise! ACLU official Barry Lynn, in a typical liberal knee jerk reaction for the poor defenseless pornographer, cried censorship. "I think the framers of our Constitution would not have wanted to create a constitutional revolution where you couldn't rap and you couldn't rock and you couldn't roll," he said.[54] Again, the parents' group had never called for censorship. They merely wanted truth in packaging for themselves and their children.

Tips From Tipper Gore and Susan Baker

Tipper Gore and Susan Baker's group hasn't given up its fight to alert parents and inform them of what they can do about obscene music. In her best-selling book, Raising PG Kids in an X-Rated Society, Mrs. Gore tells parents what they can do:

- Get to know your child's friends and their parents. Build trust.
- Share concerns and define the rules.
- Form groups to oversee and discover possible problems.

- Keep a close eye on what is happening in the music world.
- Be vocal. Talk to store owners about X-rated videos and movies.
- Use petitions to direct attention to your cause.
- Put your concerns in writing to companies, producers, sponsors, and others involved in the entertainment industry.
- Stop getting direct mail porn advertisements. Your local post office will supply you with a form 2210. Fill it out and your name will be removed from the mailing lists of objectionable advertisers.

Wanted: Christians in the Arts and Media

The technology isn't the problem. It's how the media is used. The entertainment media and the art world wouldn't be such cesspools if more people with real values would become involved.

Some of the greatest works of art and music in history were produced by Christians of past generations. Rembrandt (1606-69) is ranked as the Netherlands' greatest artist. Many of his paintings were inspired by stories from the Old and New Testament. Bach (1685-1750) wrote music in nearly every form and style known in Europe during his lifetime. A choirmaster, Bach initially wrote music for worship services.

Why aren't more Christians involved in media and art today? The basic reason is that about a hundred years ago Bible-believing church leaders developed negative attitudes toward this area of culture. To put it bluntly, in Francis Schaeffer's words, the church deserted the world of the arts.

Can you believe that only three generations ago American Christians objected to showing pictures of any kind in church? After coming to accept pictures in Sunday school books for children, they objected to pictures that "moved." When this stupidity was overcome, they fought religious dramas on grounds that players were hypocrites in taking roles other than their own.

When commercial films became popular, "thou shalt not attend a movie" became the 11th commandment in many churches and Christian schools. This is still expected in some Christian circles where it's apparently okay to watch the same movies on TV that were forbidden just a few years ago. One student at a Bible institute asked, "Why is it that I can't see a G-rated Disney film in a movie theater, while I can watch a re-run of 'Charlie's Angels' in the dorm lounge?"

Fortunately, attitudes are changing and Christians are getting back into the arts. Churches are finding that drama, for example, is an excellent aid in worship and evangelistic services. One congregation that uses drama well is Willow Creek Community Church in South Barrington, Illinois. It is the fastest growing evangelical church in America.

You can start by developing a drama group in your church or Christian school. Marti Hefley, for example, put together a group called "The New Edition," at Hannibal-LaGrange College in Missouri. The name is based on Jeremiah 31:33: "I will put my law in their inward parts and write it in their hearts . . . " The group of about a dozen students presents the gospel in drama in churches, schools, retirement homes, prisons, and many other places where the gospel is not usually preached.

Marti's husband, Jim, directs the Mark Twain Writers Conference in Hannibal, MO. "This is not a 'Christian writer's conference,'" he notes. "The conference is held on a Christian campus, but participation is open to anyone. It is named for Mark Twain, who was himself not a Christian, but grew up in Hannibal. We can learn from Mark Twain and many other secular writers."

Jim, the publisher of Hannibal Books, holds the Ph.D. in mass communications from the University of Tennessee. He is constantly urging Christians to "infiltrate" the secular media. "There are many jobs open to persons, Christians or not, with training and experience in the so-called secular media," Hefley declares.

There are also numerous opportunities in the Christian media, working for Christian radio and television stations, newspapers, periodicals, and in the book world. But the greatest challenge of the Christian media is for a wider outreach. There is still not available in America a single

Christian magazine with mass market or newsstand appeal, or a Christian TV program that will attract a mass audience.

Cheers for Christian Columnists

A number of outstanding journalists in the Christian media have made the jump to secular media. Cal Thomas is an outstanding example of one who has achieved a national readership without compromising his ideals in writing a nationally syndicated newspaper column. Here are some points made by Cal Thomas in recent columns:

- Liberals "who rail against censorship have [censored] the concepts of right and wrong from schools and from public life. [This has] produced what may be the most unethical public and private behavior ever."[55]
- "For more than 25 years, the federal courts, at the prodding of liberal special interest groups, have done their best to exclude God, morals, and ethics from public schools. It is no coincidence that this secularizing of America has paralleled the rise in drugs and crime."[56]
- In an article titled "Prison Fellowship Comforts the Dying," Thomas quotes Charles Colson: "If nonviolent offenders [in prison] could be put into work programs, community projects, and other forms of restitution, most of that money could be saved and put to use in education and other worthy projects." [57]

Cal Thomas isn't shy about reporting on the misdeeds of persons in the national media. He reported that editors from 18 major women's magazines held an unpublicized meeting to discuss whether their magazines should be used to support and maintain abortion on demand. Commented Thomas: "Gone, apparently, are all pretenses to objectivity, balance, and truth. Some of these magazines are saying to women: 'We want you to think the way we do.'" Thomas then suggested that "pro-life women might wish to send [the editors] a message by refusing to pick up their magazines in the market and canceling their sub-scriptions."[58]

In another scoop, he reported that "a march on Washington by pro-choice abortion advocates included several reporters and editors for the [liberal] New York Times and the Washington Post. None were disciplined, but executives cautioned them not to do it again. If those who report the news want to work for causes," Thomas said, "let them first resign from their beats."[59]

All of the above citations are from Cal Thomas' column as it appeared in the St. Louis Post Dispatch, one of the most liberal newspapers in America. The Post Dispatch took on the column after the newspaper was severely criticized by a number of subscribers for failing to provide balance on controversial issues.

How Christian Writers Can Penetrate the Media

You don't have to hold a full-time job in media to make your influence count. As a freelance writer, you can write and sell articles, stories, and books to both the secular and the Christian mass media. You can witness by writing about Christians who are helping people. You can address the moral side of a critical national issue. You can even "preach" through a letter to the editor or an op-ed column in which you give an opposing view to a newspaper editorial.

Don't run to the typewriter expecting to dash off a Pulitzer Prize winning story. Writing, like anything else worth doing, is a skill that must be learned. Sign up for a class in journalism or magazine writing at your local community college. Read and study Writer's Digest and The Writer, which are for sale on many magazine racks and available in libraries. Subscribe to The Christian Communicator.[60] Find markets for your material in the annual Inspirational Writers' Market Guide (available from Joy Publishing) and the Writer's Market (available in most libraries).

Join or organize a writer's club in your community. Attend one of the writers conferences listed in magazines for writers. Some are distinctly Christian in nature. Some "general trade" conferences cater to the godless, amoral

ideologies which are pervasive in the secular mass media.
The Mark Twain Writers Conference, which I spoke of
earlier, is a general trade conference which involves many
Christians. Hannibal Books also sponsors writers conferences in local churches.

The sum of it all is that we cannot change America until
we change the media. The secular mass media has gone
far, far beyond the limits of decency. The architects of our
Constitution never intended to guarantee license to
degrade and trample underfoot the values which made
this nation great. If America is to survive, there must be
a swing back to moral responsibility within the freedoms
we enjoy. The alternative is to drown in moral filth.

We must do more than curse the darkness. We must
reclaim leadership in film, music, writing, drama, and in
other arts from the pagans who now shape what
Americans see and hear in the media.

*"Lord, . . . I am your servant; therefore give me com-
mon sense to apply your rules to everything I do."*
Psalm 119:125, <u>Living Bible</u>

Chapter 7

Don't Just Stand There: Do Something

The temptation of compromise is constantly before us. We don't want to make anyone angry or displease some powerful public interest. Many of us are like the farmer in a border state during the Civil War who decided his best hope of survival was to "take" both sides. So he had his wife make a Union shirt and Confederate pants. Guess what happened when he wore them? Why, he was shot at from both sides, of course.

This way of taking a stand is like that of a modern politician running for the legislature in a rural county. When asked for his stand on a proposed new law shortening the deer hunting season, he replied, "Well, some of my friends are for it and some are against it."

"But where do you stand?" the questioner persisted.

"I stand with my friends," he declared.

Unfortunately, this man is typical of many politicians, and not a few ministers who are always checking the wind of public opinion. Take the fight to save the unborn from being murdered. For example, in October, 1989, the media reported that the pro-choice movement had the momentum. Gary Bauer, President of the Family Research Council, counted 45 Congressmen who switched from pro-life to pro-abortion. These chameleon Congressmen changed their stand to what they perceived was the view of the majority.

The Cost of Standing for Principle

Dr. Jerrell Chesney, president of Oklahoma State University for 15 years, showed greater principle in refusing to permit the showing of the blasphemous film "The Last Temptation of Christ" in his school's Student Union building. The board of regents backed him up. A group of faculty and students sued and U.S. District Judge Thomas R. Brett warned Dr. Chesney and the regents that they could be violating the First Amendment if they prohibited the showing of the film. This judge was simply following the liberal ACLU line that the First Amendment protects the worst kind of obscenity.

Instead of appealing the judge's decision, the board voted six to two, with one abstention, to allow the film to be shown. Dr. Chesney then declared, "In view of my personal loyalty to the Lord Jesus Christ I have no alternative but to resign."[61] The showing of the film went ahead as scheduled.

Another example: A Maine couple I'll call Bill and Marge took a stand when Skowhegan Area High School scheduled a school play that featured a teenage Jesus cursing, disobeying his parents, striking Joseph, getting drunk, and telling dirty stories. Bill and Marge were refused a public hearing by the school board and then ridiculed by the local press and accused of censorship. The school board not only allowed the play to be presented, but permitted it to be entered in a state drama contest.

Prepare to Fight

Get ready for battle. You will not please everybody, not even all of your friends. Expect to be criticized, perhaps in the newspaper. You might, like Dr. Chesney, have to resign your position in a company or institution, rather than compromise your principles. Or, like Bill and Marge in Maine, be exposed to public ridicule because of your stand. Whatever the cost, decide what issues are the most important, take your stand, and work for change in your church, school, neighborhood, town, county, state, and nation.

We've already noted many critical concerns in America

today, including abortion, drugs and alcohol, crime, teen-age pregnancies, pornography, divorce, problems in education, Christian bashing, immorality on TV and in the movies, AIDS, homosexual militancy, and government scandals. The list continues: homeless people, over-crowded prisons, environmental pollution, the public debt, and resurgent racism. You can probably list more than a dozen more.

Where/how will you take your stand? The Bible says we are to be "wise as serpents." (Matthew 10:16 KJV) David asked God for "common sense to apply Your rules to everything I do." (Psalm 119:125, LB) The apostle John advised his "dearly loved friends" to be careful about accepting an opinion "just because someone says it is a message from God: test it first to see if it really is." (1 John 4:1, LB) The writer of Hebrews said that a mature Christian is able to "distinguish good from evil." (Hebrews 5:14) God calls us to discern between what is hurtful and what is harmful to ourselves, our families, and our nation.

Be cautioned. Strong passions followed without wisdom can sometimes do more harm than good. Applied knowledge coupled with common sense and the principles of Scripture should shape our convictions and guide our actions.

Get the Facts

When making up your mind about an issue, ask: What does the Bible have to say about this matter? Where is it heading? What is its aim? How does it affect me, my community, and my nation?

Consider the growing practice and public acceptance of homosexuality. Homosexuals, like all other people, are loved by God. On the other hand, sexual relations with persons of the same gender are morally wrong and strongly condemned in the Bible. God created Adam and Eve, not Adam and Steve.

God's Word presents homosexuality as a perverted abnormality. The Apostle Paul speaks of women and men changing "natural" sexual relations into that which is against nature. (Romans 1:26, 27) Yet by skillful lobbying and influence in the media, gays and lesbians have made great advances while we Christians slept.

Homosexual perversion, parading under the illusion of normalcy, is harmful in many ways. It attacks the sanctity of marriage. It denies the plan of God for the reproduction of the human race. It confuses young people and hinders normal relationships. One study found that 40 percent of gay males and 39 percent of lesbians surveyed had either attempted or seriously contemplated suicide. 62

The most tragic "fruit" of homosexual promiscuity and perversion is the terrible AIDS epidemic which has become the greatest death plague in American history. This modern "Black Plague" could virtually be wiped out in a few years, and thousands upon thousands of lives saved, IF every person would simply obey the Bible in marriage and sexual relations. This is not likely to happen, because the homosexual lobbies, who refuse to admit their culpability, have been successful in brainwashing the public to believe that they are the victims of what they have caused.

What the Gays Want

Their objective is to convince the public that homosexuality is a given, natural sexual orientation. Just as some people are born to be lefthanded, they say, so we are by nature inclined to mate with the same sex. A homosexual grouping, so the argument goes, is just a natural variation among families.

In a special Winter/Spring 1990 issue on families, Newsweek devoted five full pages to family variations. The article was highlighted by a center-page color photograph showing two smiling male homosexuals relaxing beside a California home swimming pool, with their two adopted children. "Our values really are the same as those of our parents," says one of the men. "We just happen to be two men."63 Declared Newsweek: "Gay and lesbian couples (with or without children) and unmarried heterosexual couples are now commononplace." That may be true for San Francisco, but it is certainly not so in most of America. Homosexuals only want us to believe that the gay sexual orientation is as "natural" and "healthy" as heterosexuality.

Another objective is to change the language relating to homosexuals. Homosexuality has become "gay," a word once used to describe a happy, carefree life. Homosexuals do not engage in illicit sex, but follow an "alternative life style." Gays are a "legitimate minority" in the mosaic of American culture who should enjoy all the rights held by other minorities. Those who deny such rights to gays, including Christian colleges who will not hire homosexuals, are said to be discriminatory. So the perverted party line goes. So it has been gullibly accepted in many parts of society.

Gays work through politics, education, the media, and even in church conferences to attain these objectives. In 1988 a liberal judge ruled that Catholic Georgetown University must provide funds for a gay student organization on campus.

Gays apply pressure on members of the media in subtle ways. Reed MacCluggage, editor and publisher of a newspaper in New London, Connecticut, told columnist Cal Thomas that a survey found editors believing that gays deserve special protection and consideration and that "gay bashing in America should stop."

In discussing this survey in his column, Thomas noted that the newspaper industry has "failed to show equal concern about . . . readers . . . who have a conservative political or religious orientation."[64] As a public school teacher I can testify that my profession has received extensive indoctrination on gay interests from special workshops, in-service training, and teacher's guides.

The Brainwashing of Children

Suppose your fourth-grade Johnny came home and told you about a "sensitivity" time in his social science class. If that hasn't happened, get prepared. The scenario will go something like this. "Guess what, Mom. Remember when we talked about love and marriage? Well, today the teacher said that our society says its okay for some men to marry men and some women to marry women." You're supposed to swallow hard and try to act natural, as he continues spouting newly acquired information paid for by your tax dollars.

Johnny continues: "Mom, when I told my teacher about
Adam and Eve, she just laughed and said, 'That's the old
way of thinking and this is the new, progressive way.'
Mom, I didn't know what progressive meant. I put my head
down 'cause it made me feel bad." That little "sensitivity"
session in Johnny's class is directly related to lobbying
success of the public educational establishment by the
homosexual movement. Don't be fooled and don't dare sit
back and let your little Johnny be brainwashed.

Take out your Bible and give him what God says. Then
show him from history books what happened to Rome and
other empires that chose to disregard God's moral teachings.

Strategies for Action

Formulate a plan to address the erroneous teaching at
school. Don't rush off to school and begin berating the
teacher. First, sit down and prepare some strategies:

Strategy One: Clearly identify the core issue.

- What is the problem? Your son is learning a set of
  values different from what we taught him. Your
  rights as a taxpayer, parent, and citizen are being
  violated.
- How did this happen? Is the teacher pushing his/her
  own personal philosophy? Is the teacher simply com-
  plying with the authorized curriculum?
- What are some broader terms which relate to the
  issue? Freedom of religion, values, parents' rights,
  teacher rights, curriculum guide.
- Once you have identified the issue, prepare to state
  it clearly to the teacher and to anyone else who is
  involved.

Strategy Two: What are your options?

- Be satisfied that you told Johnny the teacher was
  wrong and forget the matter. If successful, this will
  solve only the immediate problem.
- Deal with school personnel at whatever level is
  necessary to make a change in the material taught.

Strategy Three: What are some possible goals in following the second option?

- For the school to teach only values which reflect those of the majority of the families in the district.
- For the school to be respectful of traditional values.
- For the school to screen all texts and remove from its curriculum any that teach unacceptable values.

Strategy Four: What actions can you take to obtain changes in the curriculum and values taught in Johnny's school?

- Present your concerns in a meeting with the teacher.
- If the teacher does not agree, speak to the principal and remind him/her of your parental rights not to have your child's home morality undermined.
- If the principal does not respond, present the problem at the next school board meeting.
- If the school board does not listen, take the matter to other parents and ask them to join you in demanding that the school be respectful of parents' rights on teachings that conflict with home values.
- Have a committee from the parents' group look into other areas where the school may be violating parents' rights.

Parents do not have to surrender their children to secularism. Parents have the right to see that their children are taught proper values. Cindy and Mark Hummitzsch, for example, became alarmed over what their daughter Laura was being taught. Before approaching the school with their concerns, they mapped out a plan of action that would allow them to oversee their child's curriculum.

At the beginning of each school year Mark and Cindy asked to see curriculum-related materials in sensitive areas. They then made an appointment with Laura's classroom teacher to present their proposal. They asked that Laura be excused from lessons and lectures in human growth and development that went contrary to their beliefs. Mark explained that they would be responsible for teaching Laura in these areas. The teacher honored their requests.

This met the need for Laura. You should consider taking the next step by organizing a parents' group. But before you make a decision, talk to other parents, confront the teacher or principal, or make demands at a school board meeting, take time to research the subject in as much depth as possible. There is nothing to be gained and often a great deal to be lost by a poor presentation.

Here are some suggestions for research:

- Read your child's textbooks. Also ask your child's teacher or the school curriculum coordinator if you can look through the teaching guides and other classroom resources.
- Contact one of the moral concerns' organizations listed in the back of this book. The Gablers have a wealth of resource material on public school textbooks. Their book <u>What Are They Teaching Your Children</u>? includes a chapter, "How To Get Better Books Into Your School and Survive."
- Ask your local Christian bookstore manager for suggestions. While there, look through publisher catalogs for books which the store can order for you. Two publishers, Christianity Today, Inc. and Hannibal Books, publish a "line" of Christian moral concern books which you can receive through the mail.
- Check the <u>Reader's Guide to Periodical Literature</u> in your public library for leads to articles in major magazines on the subject of your interest. A large library will have other indexes available for aid in your research.
- Write to organizations that keep files on issues and political candidates. League of Women Voters, Chamber of Commerce, National Association of Manufacturers, American Medical Association

Political Action Committee, Christian Action Council, National Right to Life, the Rutherford Institute
(which specializes in church/state concerns), Concerned Women for America, and Eagle Forum are
some.

- Your church denomination may have a public affairs
or Christian life office with lobbyists in Washington.
However, keep in mind that some of these offices line
up with Planned Parenthood and People For the
American Way on abortion, sexual morality, and gay
rights, to mention only three issues. The National
Association of Evangelicals and the Southern Baptist Public Affairs Committee and Christian Life
Commission does hold strong pro-family and pro-life
positions.

- Obtain information from governmental offices. Look
in the telephone book under the heading "Government" for names, address, and phone numbers of
local, state, and national agencies. When you call a
government agency, give your name and city/county,
then give the purpose of your call. Be concise and
brief. If the answer is incomplete, ask where you can
obtain more information.

- Organize and evaluate your research. Write down
points on both sides of the issue and cite references.
Look at the implications of each point.

Now you are ready to prepare a presentation. Write out
the issue again. Do a trial run with a tape recorder or a
friend. Explain and defend your position. Find strength in
numbers by uniting with other concerned groups, and
determine the kind of response you want.

Set both long and short term goals. For example, you are
concerned about a rock group that is scheduled to perform
in your child's junior high assembly. You researched this
group by watching a video and transcribing the offensive
lyrics. You believe that the school should not endorse such
language by allowing them to perform.

Your short term objective is to get this concert canceled.
In pursuing this objective, you decide to go first to the
school's assembly program committee, then the principal,

and finally the school board. Suppose you accomplish this short term objective. What further stands might you take? What long term objective could you pursue such as asking your city council for an anti-obscenity bill by which the purveyors of pornography to youth in your community can be prosecuted. Here's a step-by-step plan for accomplishing such an objective.

STEP 1: Desired Government Action:

- Arrange for drafting of pornography legislation.
- Talk to your councilmembers and their aides.
- Show them examples from your research of anti-obscenity laws that have been held constitutional in other communities.

Action:
- Inform local citizen groups of what needs to be done.
- Ask each group to designate one or two persons to serve on a community-wide steering committee for passage of the new law.

STEP 2: Desired Government Action:

- Council members volunteer to serve as co-sponsors of the bill.
- Assign representatives of the steering committee to meet with councilmembers from their districts and urge support of the bill.

Action:
- Prepare fact sheets.
- Develop a news release.

STEP 3: Desired Government Action:

- Schedule public hearings.
- Select key persons from the various citizen groups to attend and testify. Distribute supportive statements for the bill's passage to council members.

Action:
- Schedule and hold a news conference. Instructions on how to do this are presented in a later chapter of this book.

STEP 4: Desired Government Action:

- Anti-pornography bill goes to council committee.
- Meet with key community leaders to get more backing for the legislation and ask them to call their council members

Action:
- Develop letter campaign, send mailings to members, organize a citizen phone-a-thon.

STEP 5: Desired Government Action:

- Bill placed on calendar for vote.
- Meet with council members and mayor.

Action:
- Send a press release, media updates, and "alert" mailings to media and supportive persons in the community.

STEP 6: Desired Government Action:

- Bill passed.
- Write thank you notes to councilmembers who voted for it, officers of citizen groups, and to all other people who helped.
- Meet with leaders of citizen groups and appoint a watch-dog committee to monitor enforcement of the new ordinance.

Action:
- Hold a press conference and announce the watch-dog committee. Restate your position on the bill and tell why you believe it will help. Praise those who helped obtain passage.

This political action plan can be used to rid your community of many other problems. Modify it as needed.

Anti-family groups have been doing this for years. They know how to reach their objectives. Roe v. Wade, which made abortion illegal, didn't just happen. Pro-abortion activists were at work long before the Supreme Court acted to allow the beginning of this holocaust which has taken the lives of over 20 million unborn babies.

Don't be tricked by the cop-out that says politics is dirty and Christians shouldn't be involved. Politics is simply a way of getting things done. Politics only becomes dirty by actions of those involved.

Look around your community. Talk to neighbors and fellow church members. You'll find plenty of moral concerns right in your own community. You'll also find others who have been wanting to do something. Challenge them to take a stand with you and go to work.

The hour is late, but not too late. America can be changed for the better if enough people who believe in Biblical morality will just do something.

"When the righteous thrive, the people rejoice; when the wicked rule, the people groan."
Proverbs 29:2

Chapter 8

What! Me Get Involved in Politics?

Everyone agrees that it's okay for Christians to vote. We're even urged to do so by our pastors. However, eyebrows raise in many churches when you suggest that Christians become active in partisan political organizations. I know. I've been the object of such skepticism.

There's a contradiction here. We honor the founders and shapers of America. We speak of their moral convictions and ideals. We give thanks for what they did to make America the greatest nation in the world. Then we turn up our noses at involvement in politics today.

We don't stop to consider that America became a great nation because Christians and others of strong moral convictions were once involved in politics up to their necks.

Nor do many of us see the connection between Federal court decisions and citizen participation in affairs of their chosen political party. We get upset over court rules that appear to undermine Christian values. We don't stop to consider that presidents tend to appoint justices, subject to Senate approval, who reflect the liberal or conservative philosophies and platforms of national parties.

Thank God, attitudes are beginning to change. We're starting to realize that God calls us to be "salt" and "light" in all segments of society, including the political arena.

One Woman's Pilgrimage into Politics

Politics is a science, though never an exact science. To be effective in politics requires study and experience. I've worked in politics from the local precinct level to the national scene. I'm still learning how to make my convictions count. For this reason, I can relate to the political pilgrimage of Sue Mortenson.

Sue trotted off to cast her vote in the national congressional elections holding warm feelings toward the candidate who was handsome, sounded intelligent, and oozed with personal charisma. Party wasn't important to her. She couldn't see much difference between either of the major parties. She intended to vote her feelings, based on impressions received from a couple of friends whom she respected.

Her candidate was elected.

A few months later Sue became interested in news reports of Congressional debate on the proposed Child Protection and Obscenity Enforcement Act. She was concerned about the issue, but couldn't understand the actions and positions of some of the legislators, including the one she had helped elect. For one thing, she was puzzled that Senator Ted Kennedy (D-MA) and Representative Peter Rodino (D-NJ) wanted to split the bill, removing the adult obscenity provisions and passing only the child pornography part, while Representatives Dan Lungren (R-CA), Dan Coats (R-IN), Chris Smith (R-IN), and Frank Wolf (R-VA) vowed to fight for passage of the whole provision. Then she heard Dr. James Dobson, president of Focus on the Family, say, "We have been given a good law that will make it possible for prosecutors to cripple the wretched obscenity industry in the days ahead. Thank God!"

Questions began ringing in her ears. Why the tough Democratic stand to take away penalties for "adult" obscenity? Why were the Republicans vowing to fight for passage of the entire measure?

This led Sue to ask broader questions: "What makes a Democrat different from a Republican? What is the difference between liberal and conservative? Should I back the Republicans? Join the Libertarian Party? Become a Democrat? Or remain unaffiliated and simply vote for the persons who seemed to be the best candidates?" Sue decided that she needed to do some research, if she was to make an intelligent decision based on her Christian principles.

Sue found that the Republican and the Democratic parties have been the two major parties for most of our country's history. The Democratic party, symbolized by a donkey, was formed around 1830, when Andrew Jackson was president. The G.O.P. (Grand Old Party), or Republican Party, marked by an elephant, was founded in 1854 by opponents of the extension of slavery into territories that were yet to become states. In 1860 Abraham Lincoln became the first Republican president.

In further reading, Sue discovered that as the country grew and developed, the parties changed their stands on issues. Further research led Sue to conclude that most Democrats today believe in:

- Abortion rights for women.
- The Equal Rights Amendment.
- Equal rights for homosexuals.
- More government funded social programs.
- Lower spending limits on nuclear weapons and the military.

Sue noted that the Republican Party went through many changes after the Civil War. It became interested in business, farming, land ownership, and putting more emphasis on private initiative than government subsidies. She found that most Republicans today agree on:

- Prohibitions against abortion.
- Restriction of the growing power of homosexuals.
- Peace through strength.
- Less regulation and less taxes for business and individuals.
- Letting business create more jobs, not the government.
- Less government funding of social programs.

Sue looked up information on minor parties. Socialists, she found, believed in government ownership of major industries. The American Communist Party wanted a Marxist America. Prohibitionists sought the prohibition of alcohol. Libertarians wanted the government to stay out of virtually all citizen affairs. States righters wanted greater power for states.

She decided that her voice and vote could count for more as a supporter of one of the major parties. But which one? Sue found the history of both major parties informative, but she knew as a Christian she had to apply Biblical principles to these philosophies in order to decide which political party to join. To understand the differences she set out to study party platforms. She called her local library and got the addresses of the national Democrat and Republican headquarters in Washington, D.C. Then she wrote each party and requested a copy of their platform.

While waiting for replies from Washington, Sue contacted her state's Republican and Democrat party headquarters for their philosophy, goals, and objectives. To her amazement, both parties seemed to have many similar goals, such as: to help the poor, to support the United Nations, to keep up our military strength, to improve AIDS education, and to fight pornography. But she also found some major differences.

One major difference was government involvement. Both parties were concerned about social problems, but viewed government involvement differently. Democrats wanted more programs for the poor and would increase taxes to pay for these services, whereas Republicans desired a reduction in taxes and a limit on government regulation, with emphasis put on getting community organizations and individuals to help the needy.

When Sue's packets came from party headquarters she studied the "planks" of the National and State Platforms on key issues for 1988:

WELFARE
   Republicans: Provide welfare only for the truly needy.
   Democrats: Raise the minimum income level for

welfare eligibility.

GOVERNMENT REGULATION

Republicans: Cut excessive regulation.
Democrats: Increase regulation.

FAMILY

Republicans: Support the traditional family as the foundation of the social order. Encourage self reliance.
Democrats: Support all types of family arrangements, including homosexual "families." Provide more government programs for family assistance.

ECONOMY

Republicans: Support the free enterprise system with a minimum of government programs.
Democrats: Support free enterprise with more government programs.

DEFENSE

Republicans: Strive for peace through strength.
Democrats: Put more emphasis on negotiations and good intentions of other nations and less emphasis on military strength.

SCHOOL PRAYER

Republicans: Favor.
Democrats: Oppose.

ABORTION

Republicans: Back a constitutional amendment to ban abortion.
Democrats: Oppose anti-abortion amendment.

Sue compared the national party platforms with those

of her state's and found they were amazingly alike. She
underlined some of her concerns to show the difference in
the two parties. Their views on abortion were of special
interest to her.

The Democrats were officially "pro-choice." They opposed any reversal of the Roe v. Wade Supreme Court
ruling that made abortion legal. They opposed laws that
would prevent a woman from exercising her "reproductive
rights." They favored government aid to make abortion
easier for poor women. In contrast, Republicans em-
phasized both the rights of the mother and the unborn
child, favored the overturn of Roe v. Wade, opposed the
use of public revenues for abortion, and wanted an end to
government funding of organizations which advocate or
support abortions.

Sue considered remaining an "independent." This
would allow her to vote for either Republican and
Democratic candidates in an election. But she felt that by
joining a party she would have a better chance of expressing her views and helping to decide the outcome of its
platform.

After much prayer and thought, Sue decided that the
Republican Party adhered more to the Biblical principles
of government in which she believed. To join her local
Republican Party she called the county chairperson and
asked for a membership application. The chairperson then
suggested that she also write for an application and join
the state Republican Party. She did this also.

Now, just because Sue become a Republican doesn't
mean every Christian should join this party. This year Sue
may be a Republican, but next year after studying both
platforms again, she may find the Democrats more com-
patible to Biblical principles, and she'll join the
Democratic Party. Or if she moves to another part of the
country, she may find herself in a predominantly
Democratic state, where Republicans exercise limited influence. In this situation, she could decide to become active
with "conservative" Democrats. In talking with friends
from other states, she learned that some midwest
Republicans are more liberal than some southern
Republicans, while many southern Democrats are more

conservative than Northern Democrats. The ranks within the Democrat party, she was told, tend to be more conservative than the Democratic leadership on many issues.

Further exploration revealed to Sue that politicians didn't always stand on every plank of their party's platform, especially when the national party's ideas conflicted with local views. Many Democrats did not support homosexual "marriage." Some Democrats were strongly pro-life while supporting their national party on other issues. Some Republicans were actually more "liberal" than some Democrats on moral concerns.

Sue was confused by such terms as conservative, liberal, right and left wing. When she studied the terminology she found:

- The terms describe the ideological position of a candidate for office, a legislator, or a judge.
- Definitions have changed. "Liberals" once favored a free enterprise system with limited government, a position which "conservatives" hold today.
- Because a politician votes conservative on one issue doesn't mean he will vote conservative on all issues. For example, Congressman Harold Volkmer of Missouri usually votes liberal on economic matters, but on pro-life and gay issues he votes conservative.

How was Sue to decide whether she was a liberal or a conservative? John Eidsmoe, author of God and Caesar summed up things pretty well for her: "The conservative view of the limited purpose and authority of the state is consistent with the Biblical view of government, whereas the liberal view of the state has no support in Scripture."[65]

Sue knew she had a lot to learn in politics. Still, she was committed to accepting her responsibility as a Christian public citizen. She would strive to preserve the rights and freedoms for her children and grandchildren by keeping informed.

A Different Way

After making a commitment to join the Republican Party, Sue asked her friend Jane what she thought about the parties. Jane said, "I certainly agree that pro-life is the way to go, but the Democrats seem to be more concerned with the poor and environmental issues. I haven't studied the platforms the way you have, but I feel I can do more with the Democratic Party."

Jane, like Sue, had known little more about politics than her responsibility to vote. Prior to her own political involvement she heard a lot of talk about the party platform and felt embarrassed when she realized it was more than the raised floor where a speaker stood.

Now Jane realized that if she knew the party platforms, she would also know if her Congressman decided to follow his own course rather than positions of the state and national parties. She could also tell if he was favoring a special interest group rather than the opinions of the majority. She listed the following conclusions for herself and other concerned Christian citizens:

- Pay close attention to your Congressman or Senator's position on issues.
- Determine where changes need to be made in the platform. Then work to implement these changes.
- Know the pulse of your local, state, and national government.

In the meantime, Sue kept moving ahead. She volunteered to become involved in the Republican Party at the local level. The chairperson put her name on the Party's mailing list and promised to notify her of any upcoming events.

"Would you be interested in a precinct position?" he asked.

"Yes," Sue said, not knowing how difficult it often is for party officials to fill precinct positions.

After demonstrating her willingness to work, Sue was elected a delegate to the county convention. Here she was able to write resolutions for the county platform.

The next step was to become a delegate to the party's state convention where she could testify and vote to adopt the national platform, as well as help elect delegates and alternates to the national convention.

Sue's husband was now involved. They went together to the state convention and had the satisfaction of helping shape resolutions and elect people for the crucial national meeting.

Sue learned that party platforms actually originate at the precinct level where resolutions and suggestions from party members are discussed, refined, and voted upon for possible adoption. She found that before the national convention, her party, as well as the Democrats, held a number of platform sessions around the nation. She and Bill went to one of these and testified on their pro-life concerns.

Sue and Jane are typical of many Christians whom I have watched become politically involved. They're always amazed at how easy it is to become a part of the action, and sometimes they're shocked at what needs to be done.

Shaping the Party Platform

Take the experience of Mark Hammer and a group of friends who read the Wisconsin Republican Platform and discovered there was no plank on abortion. Mark told them bluntly, "I can't support this platform unless it has a pro-life stand. It's a good thing I read it." His friends agreed. They worked feverishly for two weeks to write a resolution for presentation at the state convention. Their hard work paid off. The resolution passed and was inserted in the platform.

Here's another example of individual action being rewarded. In 1989, Mary Solberg, a real estate broker from Fond du Lac, Wisconsin, found that the state Republican platform did not include a strong statement on parental consent for minors seeking an abortion. Fortunately, Mary had been involved in Wisconsin's Right to Life organization. She knew what to say and wrote a rock-solid resolution.

Mary introduced the resolution at the county level and it passed, then at the district level where it was accepted again. She and another pro-lifer wrote letters of concern to state officials. The state took action, the resolution passed and parental consent was written into the platform.

These examples can be multiplied a thousand-fold

across the country as more Christians go to work within
the political system to change America. Your voice and
influence can count as you:

- Become active in party affairs, starting at the
  precinct level.
- Convince other Christians to identify with and work
  from within their party to strengthen it.
- Educate your local citizenry on current issues.
- Recognize party problems and help implement solutions.
- Work with others in goal-setting and decision
  making.
- Support issues from the perspective of traditional
  values and Biblical ethics.
- Testify and present resolutions for improving your
  party's platform to include planks that support the
  values on which America was built.
- Stand for what you believe is right on controversial
  issues, while remaining open to hear the viewpoints
  of those who differ.
- Help select, recruit, and nominate good candidates.
- Help build strong coalitions.
- Help elect your party's candidates.
- Be prepared when an opportunity comes for service.

In 1988, I was invited to testify before the National
Republican Platform Committee on "Excellence in Education." This opportunity was presented to me because of my
involvement in the Republican Educator's Caucus. I
decided to speak on AIDS, child care, and education.
    Here are the main points of my written testimony on
AIDS as presented to the Republican Platform Committee
at its meeting in Kansas City, May 31, 1988:

   When the rights to privacy of an individual threaten
   the very survival of an entire society, the rights of
   society as a whole must take precedence over those of
   the individual. . .
   Scientists agree that the AIDS virus is the most
   serious threat to the health of the U.S. and the world

since the great plagues of the Middle Ages. No other disease in American history has posed more of a threat to huge numbers of its citizens.

AIDS is caused by a blood-borne virus that can be transmitted by semen, blood, blood serum, and bodily fluids, including, to a lesser extent, saliva. Because it is not exclusively a sexually-transmitted disease, such as syphilis or gonorrhea, its spread will not be curbed through "safe sex" alone. Hemophiliacs have contracted the disease from transfusion of contaminated blood by-products.

AIDS should be treated as a communicable disease of a life-threatening nature that poses an exceptional threat to the entire population because of the absence of any known cure. For this reason, protecting society from AIDS is a matter of utmost medical importance, and may require preventive measures of an unusual and intrusive nature.

The primary focus of concern over AIDS should be on the medical protection of society, and not on civil rights issues raised by testing procedures.

We should have routine (voluntary) and confidential testing to identify AIDS carriers. In addition to helping protect the blood supply, routine testing can also provide important data on how AIDS is spreading into the population.

My testimony on AIDS and the other subjects on which I chose to speak was combined with other views in the formulation of the party platform. The planks that emerged didn't present everything I wanted. I didn't expect that. But I believe that we got a better platform because of the information I put into the record.

More committed Christians must become active at all political levels if we are to change America. By working together we can again regain the influence in elections and legislation which was lost many years ago when Christians began dropping out of the system.

Of course, it is unrealistic to think that political involvement will eradicate every evil in America. Only God can change the heart. In the meantime, we can all put our shoulders to the wheel and work harder to change this nation.

As the Christophers keep reminding, "It is better to light one little candle than to curse the darkness."

"He who affects public sentiment does far greater service to society than he who enacts statutes."
Abraham Lincoln

Chapter 9

Get Behind a Good Candidate

My friend Jerry was telling about a "Christian" businessman who had been elected mayor in his town. "Darylann, he has everyone up in arms over the way he's been acting since election. When he ran for office he seemed to be the model Christian candidate. He was a pillar in his church, talked conservative about issues, had an attractive family, and carried a Christian bumper sticker on the back of his car."

"So, what you're telling me, Jerry," I noted, "is that he looked good, sounded good, and captured the votes, then proved not to be a good politician."

"Exactly. He won the race by a landslide, mainly because the incumbent had been linked to corruption. Once in office, our candidate proved to be self-righteous, inflexible, and almost hostile to anybody who dared disagree with him. He claimed to know the will of God on every issue and anytime the 12-member council was for an issue he was against it. His conversation dripped with Christian cliches and he came across as though he felt he was God's prophet. He was so inept and intolerant in working with individuals and the planning committees that people began calling for his removal from office. When he saw that the council was going to vote for impeachment, he resigned. He was so bad that many of our citizens are wary of any future candidate who makes a big deal of his Christianity."

I understood. It's very easy to be fooled by a candidate

who looks good and says what we want to hear. Professing to be a Christian is not enough.

How Do I Know Which Candidate to Support?

So what else is there to go on when considering which candidate to support? Russ Walton, an evangelical Christian, lists "Eight C's" as qualifications of a good candidate: Christ-centered, clean, clear, capable, constructive, consistent, courageous, and conservative. I agree with Russ. I would like to include some questions with each "C."

1. Christ-centered: Does the candidate respect God and Judeo-Christian morals and ethics? (I am using "he" generically—the candidate could well be a woman.) Is he a mature Christian? Does he control his temper? Does he demonstrate genuine concern for individuals? Does his lifestyle match his talk?

2. Clean: Are there hidden "skeletons" in his background? Is there any hint of unethical or immoral activities? Has he maintained a happy marriage? Is he family centered? Is he respected in the community?

3. Clear: Can he clearly express himself on current issues? Does he know how to integrate strong morals and ethical standards into public office?

4. Capable: Does he have the experience, education, and intelligence to qualify for the position? Is he well enough known and does he have a high enough approval rating to have a chance of being elected?

5. Constructive: Will he be an effective leader? Does he work well with other people? Is he autocratic—does he always think that he has the right answer to everything? Can he accurately discern a situation and know how to take suitable action? Can he "give" when principle is not involved?

6. Consistent: Is he same on Monday as he is on Sunday? Will election go to his head? Does he sometimes have difficulty making up his mind? When he takes a stand, will he have the commitment to follow through?

7. Courageous: Will he stand for the right when an

issue is unpopular? Can he take the heat from special
interest groups?

8. Conservative: Is he consistent in his conser-
vatism? Is he a good money manager? Are his closest
political associates conservatives or liberals?

Measure the candidate on a scale of 1-10 for each "C."
Don't allow yourself to grind a personal axe. Discern fact
from fiction. In "iffy" situations, give him the benefit of a
doubt. He probably isn't an "80"—a perfect score. But if
he's less than "50," perhaps you should consider looking
for a better candidate.

Discernment is very important in deciding which candidate to support in an election.

Don't Be Deceived By Propaganda

One of the worst feelings is to wake up after the election
and realize that you've been "had" by the winning candidate. You thought he stood for all the right things. Now
you realize that you were taken in by skillful use of
propaganda techniques.

Learn to detect propaganda appeals used to sway the
voter. Candidates may use billboards, bumper stickers,
posters, leaflets, and/or newspaper ads to present a message that appeals to your emotions rather than your
reasoning. Here are the major techniques:

- **Name-calling** gives an idea or a person a bad label.
  Nixon's opponents, for example, called him "Tricky
  Dicky." The candidate wants you to reject his or her
  opponent without looking at the evidence. Name
  calling creates negative connotations in the minds of
  listeners without providing concrete facts.
- **Glittering generality** associates an idea with a
  virtue word or phrase. Some liberals use the right to
  privacy in arguing for the right of a woman to have
  an abortion. The "right to privacy" is a virtue phrase.
- **Transfer** is a tactic by which the candidate associates himself and his position with something
  everyone thinks is good. The candidate "transfers"
  the authority and prestige of someone or something
  revered and respected to himself. He may claim to

be a law-and-order candidate. You want to know
where he stands on specifics. The most popular
transfer code word at the present time is "family."
Every candidate for office, it seems, is for
strengthening the family. The discerning party
member and voter wants to know what the candidate would do to make families stronger. Don't be
bashful about asking. Pin him down to specifics. Ask
him where he stands on homosexual "marriage."

- **Positive or negative testimonials** by famous or
  well-liked people can be used to sway public opinion.
  The candidate tailors the testimonial to the crowd.
  A negative statement from Fidel Castro would certainly help a candidate with people who do not like
  Communism. A positive testimony from British
  Prime Minister Margaret Thatcher would score a
  plus with the same folks. There's nothing wrong
  with a candidate using testimonials. But that isn't
  enough. You want to know where the candidate
  stands and how he plans to translate his ideas into
  actions.
- **Plain folks** conveys the idea that the candidate's
  message is meritorious because it is "of the people."
  Huey P. Long and other demagogues used this technique well. Liberals use this propaganda tool in
  defending their support of "people's" (translate that
  Marxist) revolutionary movements.
- **Card stacking** uses only the facts that are
  favorable to the candidate. Selected facts and false-
  hoods which have the ring of truth, along with one-
  sided, emotional illustrations can place a candidate
  in a favorable light which he doesn't deserve.
- The **Bandwagon** approach is used when the candidate recites a long list of endorsements to give the
  impression that "Everyone is supporting me in this
  election."

The discerning Christian will be aware of such subtle
political strategies. None are sufficient to qualify a candidate for your support.

How to Get the Facts About a Candidate

Where do you find what you need to know about a candidate? Look closely at his personal background and qualifications. Get the candidate's biography or resume and campaign literature, available from his campaign office. Check his scholastic achievements. A common political tactic of liberals is to paint conservatives as backward, unschooled, inexperienced, and therefore unqualified.

Scrutinize his campaign pledges. Look for specifics. Mark promises that are so general that they are meaningless.

A TV political "spot" will not provide the information you need. Attend a campaign rally and listen closely to his speech. What is he saying about the critical issues? What is he basing his opinions on? What are his goals in government? How does he intend to accomplish these goals? Do his goals line up with Scriptural principles?

Next, go to his campaign headquarters and ask his workers how they feel about him. Some responses will be biased, but you can usually get to the nub of his philosophy and goals by things said as well as things not said.

You can also pick up valuable clues from "letters to the editor" and from editorial comments in your local paper on the candidate and his campaign. Radio talk shows and public TV debates will give insights. Keep in mind, however, the overall bias of the newspaper and talk show host. Some newspapers, conservative and liberal, will support almost any candidate, no matter what his personal qualifications, so long as he shares their political philosophy. Listening and watching debates hosted by The League of Women Voters can help you nail down where a candidate stands. You may be able to call in your questions to candidates in a debate or appearing on talk shows.

For presidential and congressional candidates, information can be obtained from newsmagazines, TV, radio, Congressional Quarterly Reports, and the Congressional Record. Some magazines rate and chart the voting records of presidential and congressional candidates.

Special interest groups will provide information not

readily found elsewhere. Concerned Women for America puts out a "Political Edition" on candidates just before each national election. More helpful information on candidates can be obtained from The Conservative Caucus, Christian Voice, and from Dr. James Kennedy's Coral Ridge Ministries in Coral Ridge, Florida.

A special approach is to create a candidate survey such as the one prepared by Cindy Hummitzch in my state of Wisconsin. Cindy is the Wisconsin state representative for Concerned Women for America . Her survey helps CWA chapters in Wisconsin know where the state and national candidates stand on issues of concern to Christians. In preparing her survey, Cindy writes Wisconsin's candidates for the U.S. Senate, Congress, the State Senate, and the State Assembly. Cindy asks only 11 questions to determine where the candidates stand on abortion, pornography and other Christians concerns. The respondents need only check whether they strongly agree, agree, strongly disagree, or disagree.

Interviews and Panel Discussions

Another effective way to gather information on a candidate is through an interview. Try to interview the candidate by phone or in person, or participate in a panel interview with representatives of your church or organization. When setting up a panel discussion or public interview select a neutral place with a comfortable meeting room: in a bank, public library, hotel conference room, etc. Send a list of possible questions and other needed information to the candidates at least three days in advance. Videotape the panel discussion or interview for wider use.

During the interview,
* Ask relevant questions.
* Stick to the point.
* Ask questions that require specific answers. Not, "How do you feel about abortion?" but, "Where do you stand on the proposed bill in the State Senate that calls for parental consent before minors can obtain an abortion?"
* Ask clear questions that call for a yes or no answer.

Example: "Will you vote for a bill that sets a minimum jail sentence of ten years for persons caught selling drugs within 600 feet of a school?" An unclear question would be, "Have you participated frequently in pro-choice rallies?" "Frequently" means different things to different people. A better way to word your question would be to ask, "How many times did you participate in pro-choice rallies, two or three, four or five, or six or more?"

When you are done interviewing you should know the candidate's basic philosophy, his stand on specific issues, and his commitment to Biblical principles. You will also know if the candidate's mind, as well as his door, is open to constituency concerns.

Your church might wish to invite candidates to speak at a special meeting in the fellowship hall. Be sure to invite all of the candidates for election in your area. Have them draw numbers to see who will speak first. Give each candidate five minutes to present his positions. When all have spoken, have the candidates serve as a panel to which members of the audience can direct questions.

If this is not possible, the church moral concerns group can send letters to all the candidates, asking for their positions on special concerns of interest to members of the church. Print the answers, without comment, in a leaflet or booklet and distribute to the church. More about this in Chapter 13 on involving your church.

Call or Write the Candidate

Telephone the candidate. Get to the point. Be brief. Don't harangue or argue. You're asking the candidate for information, not preaching him a sermon. Tell him you are taking notes.

Write directly to the candidate. Ask friends to write. Individual letters are always better than "canned" correspondence. Again, make your questions specific and clear. Letters should be no more than one page in length. Write letters to the editor of local and state papers about the candidate's stance on particular matters. Skillfully written letters to the editor can sway readers and have an indirect influence on a candidate and his advisors.

Concerned Women for America suggests that you follow these guidelines in writing letters to an editor:

- Be brief.
- Say thanks.
- Don't preach.
- Ask for an answer.
- Know when to write.

I would add: Find positive ways to approach negatives. It isn't enough, for example, to criticize a school board candidate for his approval of a school-based clinic that dispenses birth control devices to students. Why not urge the candidate to support the teaching of abstinence before marriage in sex education classes? More about writing letters to the editor in a later chapter.

"Where Can I Find a Better Candidate?"

By now you may be saying, "None of the candidates have the qualities and hold the positions that I can support. My only choice is to pray that I can decide on the best of the worst." If this is the case, maybe your prayers need to be redirected.

Throughout history, God has raised up believers to speak and act for Him in government. Joseph became the prime minister of Egypt. Moses was called to lead Israel into the Promised Land. After Moses' death, Joshua was given the mantle of leadership. God challenged him to "be strong and very courageous. . . " (Joshua 1:7) During the period of the Hebrew judges, Deborah, "a mother in Israel" (Judges 5:7), was called by God to lead His people out of oppression. Many more Biblical examples could be mentioned.

The form of government in Old Testament times was different from what we have in America today. Church and state were united under a theocracy. In American democracy, no religious body should seek to dominate government. However, God still calls believers to run for public office and become involved.

Pray and ask God to show you who could run for public

office in your town or state. Maybe it's someone you know.

Ask your Sunday school class or Bible study group to join you in this prayer. As you pray that God will raise up the right candidate, urge your pastor to bring a sermon on Christian citizenship. Sitting in the pews of your church, there may be a young Joshua, Deborah, or Abe Lincoln who is thirsting for a Scriptural challenge and basis for political involvement. Maybe it's you. Prayerfully consider again the "Eight C's" of a candidate. Does a friend have these? Do you? Are either of you knowledgeable and electable? Don't excuse yourself or your friend as "just ordinary." Ordinary people committed to a platform of righteousness and morality are most needed today.

How to Influence Your Candidate

Support your preferred candidate. Contribute money. Offer your services as a volunteer worker during the campaign. He's more likely to listen to strong supporters than to people who just come around to congratulate him after election. And if he's elected, you'll be in a much better situation to influence him later than if you did nothing to help during the campaign.

The most obvious influence you can have on all candidates is to vote. Doug Wead, liaison to evangelicals for President George Bush, recently said, "Christian voters made a huge difference at the polls during the 1988 presidential election. According to the National Polling Institute, evangelicals represent 22 percent of the electorate, and 84 percent of the evangelicals voted for Bush." [66]

Visit the officeholder during the citizen hours that are held by almost every elected official. Share your concerns. Praise him if he has provided good leadership. Maintaining personal contact with an occasional visit will help your letters and phone calls have a greater effect.

Pray for your government leaders. Organize prayer groups in your church to pray for elected officials, then call your elected officials telling them you are praying for them and their staff. Follow up the call with a written letter confirming this commitment.

In my women's prayer group before an election, we pray specifically for the candidates, their health, and their families. After the election, we pray for God to guide the decisions of the elected officials.

During the 1988 Presidential race, I organized a statewide prayer chain in Wisconsin for all presidential candidates and the people involved in their campaigns.

How to Monitor Newly-elected Officials

Suppose the candidate which you did not prefer is elected. You still have a responsibility to monitor him while in office. Keep the heat on. Even if you don't persuade the candidate to change his positions, you can keep his disappointing record before the people until the next election.

What if your chosen candidate is elected? Your job as a citizen supporter isn't done yet. It's imperative that you continue to listen to what the candidate says. These are the guidelines I find useful.

- What is he saying and not saying about the current issues?
- Is he using any propaganda devices?
- What is his position, for or against, on specific issues? Is he conservative, moderate, or liberal?
- Is he maintaining his former stands on issues and working to carry out his promises?

The "New Christian Coalition"

We can have even more influence in local elections. Pat Robertson has announced the formation of a new grassroots organization called the New Christian Coalition. Ralph Reed, executive director of this coalition, says the group will focus on state and local issues rather than on national matters. Evangelicals, he says, "got it backwards in the 1980's. We tried to change Washington when we should have been focusing on the states. The real battles of concern to Christians are in neighborhoods, school boards, city councils, and state legislatures."

This new group, Reid says, will seek to reach conservative evangelicals and Catholics with three goals in mind: education on issues, creation of citizen lobbyists, and grooming of political candidates.[67]

Here's what the New Christian Coalition did recently in Pasadena, California: The city council passed a directive to pastors, asking them not to mention "particular deities or even their religion" when they opened city council meetings with prayer. The Coalition held a rally. So many people turned out, that the council reversed the directive.

The Coalition already has 25,000 members and is adding more every day. It has gained the endorsement of Beverly LaHaye, James Kennedy, Charles Stanley, and other notable evangelical Christian leaders.

The needs are out there, in our schools, neighborhoods, cities, counties, states, and nation. Good and godly candidates for office can make a difference. America can be changed one precinct, one town, one county, one state at a time. It isn't going to be easy. It calls for making sacrifices and taking risks, but it can be done.

The Legacy of a Christian Sheriff

Here's what happened in Marion County, Mississippi a number of years ago. The county had long been plagued by bootleggers who stayed in business by payoffs to law enforcement officers. Things finally got so bad that a committee of church leaders and businessmen looked for a candidate for sheriff who couldn't be bought. They settled on J.V. Polk, a Baptist layman, who with his wife operated a barbershop and beauty salon in the county seat of Columbia. "J.V.," they said, "the moonshiners are saying every man has his price. They can buy votes and stack juries. We're afraid for our children's sake."

Polk reluctantly agreed to run and with the support of the church people was elected. He had barely pinned on his badge, when a bootleg baron offered him $30,000 for protection. The barber-turned-sheriff chased him out of his office.

Sheriff Polk began making arrests, only to have juries release the violators with mere warnings. An investigation showed that many "decent" citizens were dodging jury duty. Still he kept on shutting down the illegal stills, despite threats to his life and being fired on by one moonshiner.

He gave a New Testament to every man he arrested. One man, whom he put out of business, became a Christian. A doctor at the local hospital told J.V., "Before you became sheriff, we were swamped with drinking related casualties every week end. Since you shut down the stills, our work has been reduced at least 90 percent."

Sheriff Polk finished his two-year term and went back to barbering. Mississippi law prevents a sheriff from serving two successive terms.

The moonshiners came back during the next two years and he was again asked to run for sheriff. His wife and their three teenagers pleaded with him not to run again. He told them, "I can't let the Christians of our county down. I believe God wants me to run."

After handily defeating 10 opponents, he went around to the same old places, closing down stills which his predecessor had allowed to reopen. As threats on his life became more frequent, he continued to attend church regularly. His pastor noted, "J.V. never complained, but we knew he was under a heavy burden."

One night, after making a raid, one of Sheriff Polk's deputies took him home. He was just starting up the front steps when a hired gunman opened up with a shotgun. The brave law enforcement officer who couldn't be bought died before medical aid arrived.

Over 3,000 people came to his funeral. His murder shook up the whole state of Mississippi. Citizens in other counties began demanding crackdowns on corruption.

The citizens who had backed J.V. Polk now asked his wife to run for the vacant office. Mrs. Polk hesitated, but after praying with friends and her children, she ran and was elected because "I couldn't bear to see what J.V. did go up in smoke."

She faithfully served out his term, leaving a legacy of honesty and commitment to citizen service that Marion County has never forgotten.[68]

That happened quite a number of years ago in one county in Mississippi. Think what would happen if 10,000 honest, competent, God-fearing Christian citizens should decide to run for local office in the next election.

*Unless . . . good people with pro-family perspectives
rise up to defend the values in which we believe,
there is no stopping the liberal establishment in
government."*[69]
James Dobson

Chapter 10

How to be a Citizen Lobbyist

Roger Solberg came home exhausted after a lengthy real estate meeting. As he approached the den, his wife, Mary, came storming toward him, waving the evening paper. "Will you take a look at this?" she said. "I don't believe it. Our Congress wants a raise that's more than the average American makes in one year. I'm furious!"

"What are you talking about?" Roger squinted as he focused on the article Mary was pointing at.

"The Congressional pay raise that's been proposed by a Federal Commission." Mary spat the words out in disgust. "It's going through the House of Representatives without a vote, according to Speaker Wright. I can't believe the majority of the American people are in favor of a raise that would increase salaries by $45,500 per year for some of our elected officials."

"Well, what are you going to do about it?" Roger asked, hopelessly resigned to the proposition.

"Fight back," Mary replied. And fight back she did. She was so angry she purchased a $100 ad in her local paper in Fond Du Lac, Wisconsin, explaining the issue to the public. The paper got interested in the effort and wrote a follow-up article entitled, "'Write to [House Speaker Jim Wright] About Pay Raise,' Says City Woman." Local TV and radio stations heard about the ad and called for an interview. After Mary appeared on the nightly news, her story was picked up by a Washington D.C. newspaper.

Speaker Jim Wright's power not to let Congress vote on the issue and allow it to become law so upset Mary that she took out another ad in the paper. The ad included a statement by Mary:

> As a concerned citizen, I spoke with Washington on Thursday to find out when a vote on the pay raise would occur. . . I was informed that . . . the House of Representatives, under the Iron Rule of Speaker of the House, James Wright, will not vote on the raise, thereby causing it to automatically take effect. Speaker Wright has decided not to let the issue come to the floor for a vote. He evidently feels that his job is very secure with his constituency in Texas and he doesn't have to answer to the rest of the people in the fifty states. So much for Government of the People, by the People and for the People.

Mary then asked readers to send a letter to Speaker Wright, as follows:

> Speaker James Wright
> House of Representatives
> Washington, D.C. 20515
>
> Dear Mr. Wright,
>
> As a citizen and taxpayer, I am writing to voice my opposition to the proposed pay raise. A Congress that cannot effectively deal with an outrageous federal deficit should not be rewarded with a $45,500 pay raise. I ask that you bring this issue to the floor of the House of Representatives before February 8, 1989 so that my representative has an opportunity to voice his opinion and thereby serve his constituency.
>
> Sincerely,

When Mary started her campaign against the pay raise, she didn't realize that she was lobbying.

What is a Lobbyist?

Lobbying has a bad ring in the ears of many people who visualize a high-salaried, cigar-smoking executive of some special interest group trying to woo legislative votes with campaign donations.

Despite the negative image, which is well deserved by some persons, lobbying is a respectable pursuit and an important part of the governmental process. By the simplest definition, lobbying is an effort to influence someone's decision.

You might say that Abraham was lobbying the Lord when he pleaded for mercy for wicked Sodom, where his nephew Lot lived. And that Mary, the mother of the apostles James and John, was lobbying for her sons when she asked Jesus if they could be given first place in the kingdom.

Mostly we think of lobbying in a political context. Here, a lobbyist is one who attempts to influence legislators to vote for or against a certain bill.

There are thousands of lobbyists seeking to influence state and national government. They represent companies, institutions, religious organizations, associations, and a host of other special interest groups. In this capacity they provide information on pending bills and constituent opinion for busy legislators. A conscientious legislator will listen to several lobbyists, representing different interests, before casting his vote.

A Christian Lobbyist in Action

Jack Clayton is the Washington "representative" for the American Association of Christian Schools. Jack makes it his business to keep Congressmen informed on legislation that may affect his constituency of Christian educators, board members, and students and parents.

Jack, for example, tried to point out potential problems in the Civil Rights Restoration Act (also called the Grove City Bill) which came before Congress a couple of years ago. In a prepared statement for media and legislators, he noted that the bill "drastically expands federal power over entire institutions, businesses, governments, and religious institutions if only a single federal dollar indirectly goes to it."

The bill, he said, "requires religious institutions to submit religious tenets in writing to the government for evaluation. . . . Even if a religious tenet is granted, it is wrong for religious schools to have to ask permission from the federal government to have rules governing moral conduct. . . . Why should secular officials be in a position to judge the validity of requests based on religious tenets? When did actions used upon faith become dependent on government approval?"

There is "absolutely NO clear language in the act to prevent activist federal judges from ruling IN THE FUTURE that the sex discrimination statutes must extend to protect homosexuality. In other words, the bill could require Christian schools in the future not to discriminate against homosexuals in hiring teachers."

Jack also noted a provision in the bill that said an employer "shall not make pre-employment inquiry as to the marital status of an applicant for employment, including whether such applicant is 'Miss or Mrs.'

"What does this mean?" Jack asked rhetorically. "Bigamy? Polygamy? Immoral cohabitation? Fathering children out of wedlock? These are illegal questions. Educational institutions have a right to uphold moral conduct."[70]

Lobbyists for several liberal religious denominations spoke in favor of the legislation which, unfortunately, was voted into law.

A lobbyist like Jack Clayton wins some and loses some. But he's there in Washington, representing the concerns of his Christian school constituency. Jack and other Christian lobbyists deserve our support and prayers.

How You Can Make Your Influence Felt

You don't have to be a paid, full-time "representative" of some company or organization to be a lobbyist. Some of the most effective lobbying is done by private citizens and groups who write letters to their legislators, send "letters to the editor" and press releases to newspapers and broadcast stations, telephone and visit elected officials, gather petitions, hold rallies, and testify before committees.

Lobbying is an honorable practice and by following these eight skills you can learn how, when, and where to make your influence felt:

1. Know your opposition.
2. Know the issue.
3. Follow through on each point of contact.
4. Be honest and accurate in your reporting.
5. Touch base with various coalitions.
6. Know the process. (through research at the library)
7. Be committed to your cause.
8. Avoid personal attacks.

You might begin by stating your concern in the form of a resolution, framed like this:

> WHEREAS, the Constitution of the United States does not have a pornography law.
> WHEREAS, the rights of children must be protected.
> WHEREAS, . . .

Once you have decided on the issue, plan your lobbying strategy. First, you'll need to gain local support. This may involve researching the issue, door-to-door surveys, contacting local organizations for input, interviewing community leaders, and other methods. Use ideas presented in others chapters of this book.

Once you understand the issue and get people aroused, you are ready to mobilize and lobby your state legislature.

Take a Lesson From Gay Rights' Activists

Study how other groups have lobbied on legislation. We can learn from the gay rights people. Gays are well organized and have been very successful in achieving their goals. Here's some of the strategies they follow:

- They solicit help from leaders of community "rights" groups.
- They network community organizations with infor-

mative speeches to convince people that their civil
rights are being violated.
- They create a ground swell of public support through
  marches and demonstrations for passage of a bill
  they favor.
- They work behind the scenes with supportive media
  and friendly legislators until the legislation is
  passed.

Obviously their techniques work. Can you imagine what
would happen if the Christian communities were that well
organized? If we could only tap into the 94 percent of the
population that professes faith, we could reverse the
destructive trends in society and derail the liberal agenda.

How to Lobby a Legislative Committee

As soon as your legislature opens and sessions begin,
each representative is assigned to various committees.
Committee operations and structures in state legislatures
follow somewhat the pattern of the U.S. Congress in which
the House has 22 standing (permanent) committees and
the Senate has 18. There are also four other types of
committees: (1) Subcommittees of standing committees;
(2) special and select committees; (3) joint committees
made up of members of both houses; and (4) commissions
and boards that handle special matters. The chairmen of
all committees are usually selected through the seniority
system in which a senator or representative from the party
majority who has been on the committee longest is auto-
matically elected. Some chairmen have enormous power
in setting agendas and deciding when a specific piece of
proposed legislation will be discussed and when it will be
reported out for a full house vote.
Find the answers to the following questions before you
carefully approach the committee assigned to your concern:

- What committee(s) will deal with the legislation
  related to your issue(s)/
- Who is the chairman?
- How often does the committee meet and where?
  Some committees hold hearings outside of the state

capitol.
- What committee members are working on the issue of your concern?
- How does each committee member feel about the issue? Look up speeches and campaign promises he has made. Check his voting record.
- Where do the committee members live? Who are the influentials in their areas who would support your side of the issue? Try and find at least one person from each legislator's district to lobby their representative on behalf of the issue. Representatives tend to listen best when their own constitituents speak.

Specific Approaches to Lobbying a Committee

Call the committee chairman or the particular member most identified with the issue at hand and identify yourself as a concerned constituent. Identify the issue. Tell where you live and any offices you hold. Be brief and to the point. Follow up your call with a written letter repeating your stand. Keep a copy of your letter for future reference.

Visit your district representative (whether he's a member of the committee or not) at his local office. Concisely state your concerns about the issue and suggest appropriate action for the committee. Be prepared to compromise and know ahead of time the degree to which you can agree to give ground. Be polite, courteous, and brief. If several persons accompany you, choose a principal spokesperson and decide what each member will address. Above all, be on time and don't overstay your welcome. Fifteen to 30 minutes should be sufficient time to get your point across.

If you desire to address an open committee hearing, make a written request to the committee or subcommittee chairman, or the minority leader of the legislature. Inform your district representative of your intent and solicit his assistance. After being accepted, check with your representative's office for the correct format of your testimony, prepare carefully, and make at least 50 copies for submission to the committee 48 hours before you testify.

Seek legal advice on matters about which you are un-

certain. If there's a national organization which shares
your concern, call their office and ask for assistance. Many
attorneys, for example, stand ready to assist state and
local groups in the pro-life movement.

Enlist others to testify and attend the committee hearing. Be sure that the testimonies are well prepared and to
the point of the matter at hand. Have four or five people
ready to give impromptu testimony, should time permit
the chairman to throw the floor open for anyone else who
wishes to speak. Instruct each of your speakers to avoid
character attacks on opponents. This can damage your
influence and could even result in a nasty defamation
lawsuit.

See that each of your supporters wears a badge or some
marker which plainly identifies him or her with your
group and its position on the issue. The legislators need to
know that your group is there in force.

Here's how this was handled by a group of Missouri
parents concerned about proposed legislation that would
greatly restrict home schooling. Two women in the group
marked a standard-sized piece of typing paper into
squares and drew a sketch of a house in each section. They
then made copies and cut out a house for each person
attending the hearing to wear on their lapel. When the
hearing began, committee members had no trouble recog-
nizing that most of the people present were with the home
school group.

Don't Stop Now

Committee hearings and deliberations are only part of
the process. After the committee votes, the proposed legislation will be taken up by the full assembly.

The same procedures apply as before. Instead of lobbying individual committees, you will be seeking to influence
the representatives who were not in the committee.

Divide these legislators into three groups according to
their known positions and voting records:

- Those who are clearly on your side.
- Those who oppose your position and are not likely to
  change.

- Those who have a mixed record and tend to test the wind of popular opinion before voting.

The first group will bear watching to see that none are pressured to vote for your opposition. You might pick up a vote or two from liberals in the second group who come from districts with a sizable conservative vote—if persons from their district contact them. You'll probably want to spend most of your time lobbying the swing group. Quite often, this is the group which you must impress and influence if you are to win.

Here are some activities which will might help you gain votes:

- Rallies. Recruiting people from every district and holding a rally at your state capital will draw attention to your cause. Send a press release on the rally to media. Follow up with personal calls to media persons whom you want to be there. Before the rally, ask those in your group to stop by their respective representative's office.
- Picketing. An orderly demonstration can generate support for your cause. Carry signs bearing messages clearly identified with the issue. Do not shout back at hecklers. Sing appropriate songs. Chant meaningful slogans. Who can ever forget the chants in the April, 1990 pro-life rally in Washington as thousands of people challenged the media to "Tell the truth! Tell the truth!"
- Form coalitions. Work with other lobbyists and organizations. You can gain support by helping others. Evangelicals need Catholics, for example, and vice versa.
- Hold open hearings around the state and in the state capital. As with rallies, notify the media and also invite county and local officials to attend. Use a small room and have plenty of copies of your statement and agenda to share with everyone there.

Remember that a piece of legislation must be passed in identical form by both houses of the state legislature or

Congress before it is sent to the chief executive. When the houses of a legislature pass different versions of the same bill, a special conference committee is convened to iron out the differences. This provides an opportunity for you to lobby committee members for changes in some of the most objectionable parts of the legislation.

The object of your lobbying is to get votes. If you do a good job, you may be surprised at some of the votes. Did these legislators "see the light" or "feel the heat?" You may never know whether they were "true converts" to your cause or not. Whatever, you are called to be faithful to the job God puts before you.

Win or lose, your job isn't over after the final vote is taken. Thank those legislators who voted the right way. Express regret to those who voted the other way. Tell them that they will be hearing more from your group, and that you are not going to fade away into the sunset.

Don't Forget the Governor

A piece of state legislation isn't law until signed by the governor, as it isn't law in Washington until the president affixes his signature.

The governor will have a certain number of days to make his decision. He can sign the bill and let it become law, or he can decline to sign it. In the latter case, the legislature may try to overturn the governor's veto by seeking a two-thirds vote.

It's vitally important that the governor know where your group stands. Have supporters of your cause write or call the governor's office, urging him to take the action your group desires. He, like any other elected official, is interested in what you have to say. Also, he may need your vote in the next election.

Use the media to get the governor's attention. Give your response to the media about the law awaiting the governor's signature. Make yourself available for an interview. The TV station or newspaper may already be in touch with your opponents. They will be glad to have a countering view on the issue.

How to Lobby Your Congressman

Your congressman, especially if he won by a small margin of votes in the last election, wants to keep up with the opinions of his constituency. If 75 percent or more of the voters in his district favor a bill, he will support that bill. Without input from his constituents, he will be forced to follow his own judgment and that of his political "eyes" and "ears" in the district. Before you contact your congressman or any other elected official, prepare a fact sheet on him as suggested earlier. Once you understand his record and the legislation in question, you're ready to approach your representative by letters, phone calls, and in other ways previously noted.

Send copies of your correspondence and replies from your congressman to the national office of the organization which represents your cause in Washington.

Make Your Voice Heard Across the Land

There are critical issues before us in our states and nation. We must become involved as citizen lobbyists. List these concerns on a sheet of paper as they come to mind. Then go back and number them according to your priorities for changing America. Pro-life may be at the top of your list.

Would it shock you to know that America has fallen below zero growth in native-born population. More Americans are dying than are being born.

Millions of unborn babies are lawfully murdered every year. A writer in <u>Newsweek</u> magazine proposes that the population be reduced further by having the government pay every pubescent girl $400 for not getting pregnant for one year. The second year she would get $500, then $600 the third, and so on until she is 52 years of age. If she chooses never to bear any children, she would receive almost $100,000 for her non-productivity.

Humanist social reformers are also calling for laws that will allow doctors to hasten the death of elderly persons who are ill. We are told that because people are living longer lives, the elderly will soon overtax the support system of social services. We are warned that there may come a time when younger adults will demand that the lives of the older generation be shortened.

What next? Will parents in the next generation be legally permitted to put undesired or troublesome children to "sleep" in the fashion of present veterinary practice? If you don't think this is impossible, read and think about the following imaginary letter sent to the American Family Association from Save-A-Life in Macon, Georgia. It is dated January 22, 2023.

Dear Mom:

Can you believe it's 2023 already? I'm still writing 22 on nearly everything. Seems like just yesterday I was sitting in first grade celebrating the century change!

I know we haven't really chatted since Christmas. Sorry. Anyway, I have some difficult news and I really didn't want to call and talk face-to-face.

Ted's had a promotion, and I should be up for a hefty raise this year if I keep putting in those crazy hours. You know how I work at it. Yes, we're still struggling with the bills.

Timmy's been "OK" at kindergarten although he complains about going. But then he wasn't happy about day care either, so what can I do?

He's been a real problem, Mom. He's a good kid but quite honestly he's an unfair burden at this time in our lives. Ted and I have talked this through and through and finally made a choice. Plenty of other families have made it and are much better off.

Our pastor is supportive and says hard decisions sometimes are necessary. The family is a "system" and the demands of one member shouldn't be allowed to ruin the whole. He told us to be prayerful, consider ALL the factors and do what is right to make the family work. He says that even though he probably wouldn't do it himself, the decision really is ours. He was kind enough to refer us to a children's clinic near here, so at least that part's easy.

I'm not an uncaring mother. I do feel sorry for the

little guy. I think he overheard Ted and me talking about it the other night. I turned around and saw him standing at the bottom step in his pj's and the little bear you gave him under his arm and his eyes sort of welling up.

Mom, the way he looked at me just broke my heart. But I honestly believe this is better for Timmy, too. It's not fair to force him to live in a family that can't give him the time and attention he deserves. And PLEASE, don't give me the kind of grief Grandma gave you over your abortions. It's the same thing, you know.

We've told him he's just in for a vaccination. Anyway, they say the termination procedure is painless.

I guess it's just as well you haven't seen that much of him.

Love to Dad.

Jane[71]

Are you saying, "That couldn't happen in America?" If things keep going in the present direction, don't be sure that it won't. Would your grandmother have believed 40 years ago that a million-and-one-half pre-born babies would be killed this year alone?

We simply can't afford to take the risk of things getting worse. More of us have got to get off our duffs and get involved in the political process now. One way to do this is by lobbying.

"When bad men combine, the good must associate; else they will fall, one by one, an unpitied sacrifice in a contemptible struggle."
Edmund Burke

Chapter 11

How to Organize an Effective Citizens' Group

"I know not what course others may take; but as for me, give me liberty, or give me death!"

Patrick Henry's cry rings of personal commitment. But it wasn't enough to win independence for the United States of America.

The 13 independent colonies had to join together in a "citizens' group" for liberty, for as shrewd Benjamin Franklin declared, "We must all hang together or assuredly we shall hang separately." Congregationalists, Baptists, Methodists, Presbyterians, Lutherans, Catholics, and others sent their elected representatives to the Continental Congress.

The Continental Congress proclaimed a Declaration of Independence in which they presented their reasons for breaking ties with Mother England: "We hold these truths to be self-evident... We mutually pledge to each other our Lives, our Fortunes, and our sacred Honor."

Our forefathers won the Revolution by forming a national citizens' group—a coalition of concerned patriots, if you please. They fought together to establish a new nation "with liberty and justice for all."

A new moral revolution is desperately needed today. To lead that revolution we must have coalitions of like-minded citizens who will band together and lead America into a new era of spiritual freedom.

That's what this chapter is about—how to form an effective citizen's group that can join other groups in a wider coalition to change America.

The General Planning Stage

"... To be prepared is half the victory."[72] Unfortunately, Don Quixote didn't live up to his declaration. He attacked windmills he thought were giants and flocks of sheep which he mistook for armies. He wasn't really prepared. He didn't know what he was doing.

To keep your group from tilting at windmills, you must plan well. Start with a concern. You're not organizing a citizens' group or coalition just for exercise. The battle can only be won by a number of citizens working together. If you've read the early chapters of this book, you already know of many needs which beg for solutions. It's likely that you don't need to look elsewhere; the need is already upon you and you want to do something about it.

The problem could be a drug epidemic in your town, pornography easily available to children in local stores, corrupt law enforcement, an abortion mill down the street, or family life curriculum in your child's school that takes no stand on sexual abstinence.

Maybe you've tried to deal with the problem by yourself or with a small group from your church. You got bloodied and ridiculed for the effort. You're determined now not to be defeated again and have decided to get more people into the fight.

Before mounting your horse and riding off to corral the enemy, take a survey. This will show you if enough people really care about the problem.

Before you prepare the first form and make the first contact, answer these basic questions:

- What is the purpose for the survey?
- What am I trying to find out?
- How am I going to do it?
- What are the boundary lines from which the information is to be obtained?
- Who should be included and who should be excluded?

- How many should be interviewed, everyone or just a representative sample?

There are no magic formulas for constructing a survey form, but there are some necessary ingredients: carefully worded questions to avoid confusion, direct and simple questions requiring short answers, and open ended questions which will allow persons to draw and express their own opinions.

For easy tabulation, ask, "Do you Agree, Strongly Agree, Disagree, or Strongly Disagree with the statement that . . . " Another effective method uses a 10-point scale rating system with "0" being the worst and "10" the best.

The majority of people will likely not be able to identify the real problems. They may only reflect what they see on TV or read in the newspaper. The media sets the agenda for what many people think about and talk about. Keep this in mind when framing your questions.

Before developing the final draft, have two or three close friends or co-workers read the survey to check for clarity. In this way, you can correct mistakes and sharpen up the survey before printing.

Whether you do a door-to-door, mail, or telephone survey, you'll probably want to survey only a representative sample. How do you choose a sample that is representative?

Telephone Surveys

For a telephone survey sample, simply mark every "nth" person in the directory. An even simpler way is to call the people at the top and bottom of each page. This method will not be exactly representative since many persons have unlisted phone numbers. Sophisticated survey researchers use computers that dial a sample of numbers to reach the total telephone population. A simple sampling method will probably be sufficient for your purposes.

When you call, first identify yourself or your group by name. Explain why you are calling and politely ask, "Do you have a couple of minutes to answer a few short questions about this concern?" Don't be intimidating or pushy. Most people will respond politely if you are polite to them.

A prepared telephone script is the easiest method to follow.

Door-to-Door Surveys

These work best on weekends when people are outside in their yards or doing leisure activities with the family. The best time is between 9:00 a.m. and 4:00 p.m. on Saturday, or on Sunday afternoon. Dress neatly but casually and always wear a smile. Walk in two's. Never enter a home alone. Knock or ring the doorbell; if no answer, write the address on the sheet and return later.

Tell who you are and who you represent. Explain the survey. Say that you want their opinion and that all responses are kept confidential. Never put anything in a mailbox—it's illegal. It is advisable to have the person fill the form out immediately, before you move on to the next house. Don't leave surveys to be filled out at the respondent's leisure. Returning to pick them up creates extra work, and even people with the best intentions forget and misplace the forms.

Mail Surveys

If you can afford to do so, take a mail survey. You can take a sample from the city directory, using every "nth" name or the names at the top and bottom of each page. To encourage a reply, enclose a postpaid return envelope. Many people don't even write to their own "Aunt Helen," so don't expect a high return. A 30 percent reply can be sufficient.

After You've Done the Survey

You've completed the survey and have found that a sizable number of people are concerned about the problem. Now you're ready to take the next step.

- Start by calling five to eight key people whom you already know will be "with" you. Invite them to meet in your home or another place. Follow up with postcard reminders. This ad hoc group can serve as the temporary executive committee until you have the first formal meeting of a larger group.

- Research the problem well before the meeting. Talk with local clergy. Look up related articles at the library. Meet with elected officials. Write up a summary of the survey results and what you learned elsewhere. Make a list of things that should be done. Copy and have all material ready for distribution at the first meeting. Be sure to prepare an agenda before the meeting.
- Begin with a welcome. If they don't know one another, introduce everybody and take a few minutes to get acquainted. Then pass out the results of your research and the survey and ask everyone to take a few minutes to read it through.
- Next, lead the group in drafting a simple consensus statement which sets out what the group wants to accomplish, such as, "This concerned citizens' group will attempt to do something about the drug epidemic in the city of Plainville."
- Ask a "temporary executive committee" to draft some tentative goals and a step-by-step action plan which will be needed to reach these targets. This need not be fancy. The plan can be reworked and approved by the organized group at a later date.
- If you think the group will be permanent and will address issues which will gain attention from a wide audience, then write down some tentative bylaws and share information on tax exemption and incorporation. You may wish to seek advice from a sympathetic attorney on such matters.
- Decide on a name for the group, which you will present for a vote at the first formal meeting. The problem which you are attacking should be prominent in the name.
- Decide on a time and place for regular meetings, at least for the next six months. A private dining room in a local restaurant, the YMCA, a school room, and a room used for public meetings in a union hall or business are all good places to meet, assuming that seating is adequate. A church hall might be suitable if nothing else is available. It's probably best, however, not to meet regularly at one church, especially

if you want to involve a large cross-section of people.

The First Meeting

Plan an interesting program. Announce that you'll be forming "The Coalition to Rid Our City of Drugs" or whatever title you have chosen. Schedule a speaker and/or panel discussion, but make the main course on the menu the organization of the coalition.

Publicize! Publicize! Publicize! Tell what your group proposes to do. Send out news releases, which include the names of the temporary executive committee, at least a week before the meeting. Hand deliver releases to local news outlets. Send public service announcements to local radio stations. Invite media to attend the meeting and have reserved seats awaiting at a table near the front. You'll find more help on how to use the media in a later chapter.

Notify organizations with kindred concerns. Provide bulletin inserts for cooperating churches to distribute at Sunday services. Send special letters of invitation to VIPs, clergy, elected officials, lawyers, bankers, presidents of service clubs, etc. Ask them to pass the word on to others.

How to Conduct a Fruitful Meeting

Start on time and follow a prescribed agenda. Adopt a standard book on parliamentary procedure such as Robert's Rules of Order.

Have the temporary secretary of the organizing committee take notes. Recognize special people such as elected officials, clergy, and leaders in other organizations. State why you are organizing.

At the next meeting, the presiding person should promptly call the meeting to order. Have the temporary secretary read the minutes from the previous meeting. Next, the presiding officer will ask the chairman of the nomination committee to present the committee's nominations. After other nominations, if any are taken from the floor, a vote is taken. The duly elected chairman or president will then take charge and follow the agenda for the remaining of the meeting.

The person presiding should now review the purpose statement and introduce the bylaws for open discussion and recommendations.

Announce the time and place of your next meeting.

Introduce the guest speaker or the people on the panel who will talk about the main concern for which the group is being organized. The length of time allotted for program activities should be clearly indicated on the agenda.

Allow no more than 25 minutes for a speech, 10 minutes of video, 15 minutes of discussion, 10 minutes of wrap-up, then close with prayer for the group's concerns and plans for the future. Nothing will dampen enthusiasm faster than a dragged-out meeting with long-winded speeches and prayers. The chairman should take action when necessary. Dwight L. Moody, the practical-minded evangelist, once requested in a meeting, "Mr. Sankey, will you lead us in a hymn while our brother finishes his prayer."

Allow at least 10 minutes for questions and comments from the audience.

Close on time.

The best intentions can come to naught if meetings are not well planned and executed. First Corinthians 14:40 is worth keeping in mind: "Everything should be done in a fitting and orderly way."

Your citizens' group will want to work with other groups pursuing the same purpose. This can be done without formal linkage, although it is helpful to elect one person or a committee who can interact with representatives of other groups in coordinating efforts. However, cooperation should always be voluntary in a coalition.

Each local group or coalition can learn from the others. What works in one city can succeed elsewhere. On state or region-wide projects, groups can take common stands. The larger the number, the greater the influence of the coalitions in politics and the media.

Communicate. Communicate.

Communication will prevent misunderstandings from developing and will keep members of your group aware of what is happening and fired up for action. Communication will also cut down on the number of meetings required to get a job done.

How you communicate will depend upon your project and how frequently your members need to be given information. Many coalitions mail their secretary's reports to the members, use a telephone hot-line for special alerts, or send a weekly or monthly newsletter to keep members informed. Your group may wish to use a combination of methods.

When to Have Paid Employees

Unless you have extraordinary resources, don't start off with a paid staff. If your group or coalition has more than 200 members, you might consider renting an office and employing a paid part-time secretary or coordinator. As the membership and work load increases, other staff members can be added.

As your group grows larger and becomes more involved, a lobbyist may be hired or shared with another group to provide representation in the state capital when the legislature is in session.

Continuing Education is Essential

Because of our fast-paced society, many concerned people don't have the time to do extensive research. If your group provides well researched and documented information, pastors, educators and legislators will seek to be informed.

These three methods are proven ways of keeping your members and visitors educated and informed:

1. Prepare members to be become better informed at meetings. In the fall of 1988, Pam Peterson, the Wisconsin legislative liaison for Concerned Women for America, and I put on a state-wide leadership conference for CWA. Our purpose was to develop leadership skills in women and inform them on the legislative process at the state and national level. As in the general meetings, each participant received a packet containing an agenda, hand-outs, note paper and pencil. Since this was a training seminar, we

decided to use the lecture format. We both spoke on different topics for approximately 45 minutes each. We allowed one hour at the end of the day for questions and answers, to allow for audience participation.

2. Provide advance information. Inexpensive and sometimes even quantities of free material can be obtained by contacting your local library's reference section, your State Representative, Congressman, or the U.S. Senate office in your district. Information can be organized, summarized, and typed up, then copied for handouts to members.

3. Use small discussion groups for maximum participation. The four most frequently used discussion methods are described below. Vary them to stimulate involvement and add variety to your meetings.

- For a panel discussion, the chairman briefly outlines the topic, then serves or appoints a moderator for a panel of three to six people to discuss the topic and related issues. The moderator sees that all panel members have the opportunity to speak. After a designated period of time the moderator asks members of the audience to contribute or to ask questions of members of the panel. A panel discussion can be quite effective following a lecture. After the speaker finishes, the panel members react. Members of the audience are then asked to present their views.
- The format for a symposium is similar to a panel discussion, except that each participant presents a certain part of the subject. The chairman maintains control and helps facilitate audience participation.
- In a debate, the participants present different points of view in an argumentative fashion. A person who is opposed and even antagonistic to the views of your group may be challenged to debate. He should be treated fairly and with courtesy. During a debate, the time keeper is seated to the side of the debaters and allows each a three to five minute speech, a one minute rebuttal, and a three minute wrap-up, although time limits can be longer. The winner is determined by judges or by metered audience applause.

Workshops and Conventions

As your group expands, you'll need more expanded programs. The next step might be to sponsor a day-long workshop at a convenient site. Choose the site and book the leaders at least six months in advance. Depending on the projected attendance, you will probably have several groups meeting at the same time for maximum participation. Repeat the most popular workshops so all who wish can attend.

A convention obviously requires much more planning. It will include exhibits, plenary sessions, and satellite meetings of special interest groups. Your committee should start planning at least a year or more in advance. Most hotels require that rooms be reserved, with deposits, a year in advance for a convention and three months for individual registration. Request information from convention bureaus in several cities. Travel distance, lodging, parking, and meal costs are some of the items to consider in comparing costs. Before selecting a site, your chairperson and others in the group with specialized responsibilities should visit the cities. They'll need to check the size of the hall, acoustics, adjacent meeting halls, and platform setup.

Two or three people should not try to do all the work in setting up a workshop or convention. Your chairperson and chairs of various committees need to be involved in the decision making and planning processes. In planning a state political convention, I held bi-weekly meetings with my co-chairpeople and executive committee. I also included them on the tour of the convention hotel and discussed the contract for the facilities, the estimated cost, and the theme for the convention. We met months before the convention and kept everyone informed with minutes of our meetings.

A smooth-running convention will require several committees to carry out various functions. Possible committees include finance, publicity, set-up, clean-up, program, printing, registration, decoration, hospitality, and press relations. Detailed check lists should be prepared for each committee chair.

After the convention, or any function sponsored by your group, express personal gratitude to each person who helped. Send a simple "thank you" card with a short note thanking the volunteers for giving their time and encouraging them to continue helping in the future.

You Can Do It In Your Neighborhood

Right now you're probably thinking, "Me, organize my neighborhood? This is all beyond me, I'm not capable." Or maybe you're like one husband I know who keeps saying, "I'm not a fighter, and besides, it won't do any good anyway." Well, let me tell you about two young women from the midwest who decided to be involved and make some changes in their neighborhood.

Coming from a small middle-class community, Brenda and Laura decided to get involved in their kids' futures now. They wanted to be on top of what was happening in their neighborhood before big problems, such as drug use, arose. They started asking around and found other mothers who were concerned enough to start a "Neighborhood Concerned Citizens' Group."

First they asked people in a six block radius if they would like to be involved. As they canvassed door to door, they listened carefully for any possible concerns. Were the streets adequately lit? Were they clean? Any vacant lots or abandoned buildings? Any objectionable businesses in the neighborhood? They made a list of people's concerns and ideas for community improvement. They made a special note of women who could articulate well.

Next, they went to the city clerk's office and got voting precinct boundary sheets. They used these to determine the size of the district and the educational, social, and political make-up of the neighborhood.

They checked with the Chamber of Commerce and others to see if there were any other coalitions in the district. Finding none, they chose a small community hall with good parking for their meeting. Since many potential members had small children, they hired two local teenage girls to provide babysitting in a room off the main hall.

Then they put together a short news announcement on a single sheet of standard sized paper and distributed it to all the households. Two weeks before the meeting they gave a news release to their local paper and asked their local radio station to make a Public Service Announcement about the meeting.

"The meeting ran smoothly because we were organized," said Brenda. "We put the agenda on every chair in the room so when people arrived they could see what was going to happen and be ready to respond."

"We knew we had to look professional or the people would not come back," Laura added. "So we followed Robert's Rules of Order to a 'T.' We had our suggested name for the group posted on the wall, our purpose statement on the blackboard, and our organizational structure written on two large tag boards.

"After we voted on the name and completed the general business, we decided on what committees we would need and if we wanted a membership fee. An attorney in the group volunteered to check state regulatory law to see if we needed incorporation status.

"Before concluding the meeting we set a permanent time and place for future meetings and decided on a method of keeping the members informed. Then we promptly adjourned, as the agenda indicated, at nine p.m."

Brenda and Laura knew, however, that as organizers of the group their job wasn't done. Between the two of them they had to build community support. They went to the Chamber of Commerce and asked for a book listing all the clubs and business groups in the city. Then they began attending the various meetings in hope of forming an alliance with them. "We knew if we offered them help on a project, then they in turn would offer us help if we needed it," Brenda related later.

At their second meeting the group came up with it's first challenge. "We chose a minor problem because we wanted to see if our strategy steps would work," Laura reported. "We decided to see what we could do about the battered trash cans lining the street. We notified the local media and got a group out on a Saturday to paint the cans and replace some of the worst ones. Not only did parents participate; they brought along their children. That night we made the prime time news."

Painting and replacing trash cans may seem like a tiny, unglamorous thing to do in trying to change America. But for Nancy and Brenda's group, it was a start. Their next project will be more challenging. They will take it on with full confidence that by working together it can be done.

Ready, Set, Go!

You can do something too. Stop complaining. Look around and see what needs to be done in your own neighborhood. Take your cue from Ecclesiastes 9:10: "Whatsoever your hand finds to do, do it with all your might." Enlist neighbors and get them excited. Remove "can't" from your vocabularies. Go forward in the spirit of Edgar A. Guest:

> *"He started to sing as he tackled the thing*
> *That couldn't be done, and he did it."*

America can be great again if enough citizens band together to change their neighborhoods.

"All I know is what I see in the papers."
Will Rogers

Chapter 12

Making the Most of the Media

Myron F. Boyd once said, "A half-truth is a dangerous thing, especially if you have hold of the wrong half." How true. Earlier we discussed the negative aspects of the media, but fortunately, we can effectively use the media to our advantage.

Let's first break the media down into three areas: personal, supportive, and public.

Personal media includes newsletters, correspondence, and other forms of communications which you produce yourself or have produced within your coalition.

Supportive media is comprised of Christian publications, press associations, and broadcast stations which have as their primary purpose the promotion of the Christian faith and civic righteousness. These media are vitally interested in news which is of national interest and relates to the family. Some are independent, while others are affiliated with denominations and Christian organizations such as Focus on the Family and Concerned Women for America.

The public media includes newspapers, secular magazines, and radio and TV stations. Because the public media has a much higher audience than Christian media, it is of the utmost importance that we know how to relate and deal with it in order to accomplish our purposes in restoring America to the moral greatness it once knew. Thus, the emphasis of this chapter will be on using the public media, which for publicity purposes, includes Christian newspapers, periodicals, and broadcast stations.

The public media, at least in theory, is supposed to be fair to Christians and America's Biblical heritage.

Why Christians Often Fail in the Media

Why is Christianity and America's Biblical heritage so misrepresented in the media? One reason is the ignorance and bias of many in the secular media in regard to our heritage. Another is that many Christians simply do not understand how the public media works.

Typically, a Christian organization will hold a convention or workshop featuring an array of interesting speakers and leaders. When nothing is mentioned about the meeting in local media, the leadership simply assumes that they were deliberately shut out. This is not necessarily true. It often happens that the media was not properly informed.

For many years textbook analysts Mel and Norma Gabler wondered why their opponents were getting all the press on debates over public school textbooks. Every year the Gablers testified before the Texas State Board of Education and Textbook Review Committee at annual public hearings on adoption of textbooks for use in Texas public schools. Every year the Gablers would read only the views of the other side in newspaper stories. In desperation, Mel and Norma went to their sympathetic local newspaper editor and expressed their frustration.

"Have you been sending out any news releases?" he asked.

Norma stared at him in puzzlement. "News releases? What's that?"

"If we don't know what's going on," the editor explained, "we can't put anything in the paper."

How the Gablers Got in the News

Taking tips from their editor friend, the Gablers learned how to prepare releases of their positions on objectionable textbooks which they intended to make at the annual hearing. They sent these to Texas newspapers and broadcast stations, the AP and UPI wire services, and other media. Their side was heard when they learned to be assertive and not wait for the media to come to them.

The Gablers also learned how to get attention from the press when testifying before educational authorities. One year Norma wrapped several objectionable books in brown paper and marked them "X-rated" because of immoral content. One book, she noted, even suggested that incest could be "creative." Her remarks got wide attention across Texas. A newspaper headline declared: "Mother Protests 'X-rated' Textbooks." The "X-rated" books were rejected by the review committee.

At another hearing Norma held up a fifth-grade history book that gave seven pages to Marilyn Monroe, while mentioning George Washington only eight times (and then without telling about his accomplishments). Norma quoted a paragraph about Ms. Monroe: "As Norma Jean [her original name] grew older, the boys noticed how pretty she was. When she walked down the street, men turned to watch her. . . . . She was pretty. She seemed to know just how to stand and pose."[73]

"What does this have to do with history for fifth-graders?" Norma Gabler asked. The media got the message and so did school officials.

None of this probably would have happened if they hadn't become assertive and taken their side to the media.

Building Bridges

Surveys have shown that a large percentage of media people travel in liberal circles and do not attend any church. Many are simply not aware of the growth and influence of evangelical Christianity. They tend to stereotype evangelical Christians as narrow-minded fundamentalists and blind followers of opportunist ministers. The television ministry scandals have served to reinforce this view.

Unfortunately, some of this is true. We are faced with the challenge of cleaning up our act and changing the image of evangelicals before the media.

In general, here's what we must do:

- Be believable. Unfounded opinions will destroy your credibility and that of your organization. Most media will not be burned twice after being given erroneous information. Present the documented facts in logical order. Be fair to the other side. Present both sides of a story. Avoid pejorative language. Keep anger out of your copy.
- Be available. Offer to be a source for future information. When I came back from a White House meeting of the Republican Educators, I called Barbara Schmits of my local paper in Oshkosh, Wisconsin, and told her about their future plans. I wanted conservative public school teachers in the area to know about the Rebpulican Educators, and how they could get involved. Barbara gave me a good feature article.
- Be open. Don't pre-judge media representatives. I remember dreading an interview with one liberal newspaper journalist whom I was sure would nail me to a cross for my beliefs. Not only was I dead wrong about the journalist, but he gave me a fair, quarter-page story. This taught me not to form preliminary opinions about media people which are not based on facts.
- Build friendships with reporters. Learn their names and hand deliver your material whenever possible. Leave your shoulder chips at home. Don't draw the reporter into an argument. If the reporter differs with you, be respectful of his or her opinion.
- Be gracious. Call and thank a reporter for articles you feel were written well. Express appreciation for printing anything you have written, even if you feel you were short-changed. Don't be offended by minor editing or the brevity of a feature in the paper or on TV. If you feel that something was omitted of significant importance, call and courteously ask why. An editor may have removed a key fact or quote in trimming the piece. Don't be accusatory. Don't lose your temper. Don't blame a reporter for a headline which was written by someone else on the paper. Display an attitude of wanting to learn. Clarify

something that may have been misunderstood. Give the reporter the benefit of a doubt. If you feel that the paper or broadcast station has been grossly unfair to you or your group, ask for the privilege of presenting an op-ed statement.

Use Public Service Announcements.

If your organization is non-profit and you have something to say or announce that is of public interest, send public service announcements to local TV and radio stations. Both announcements are the same except the TV message uses visuals, and radio, of course, does not. Newspapers will also print PSAs.

If you are not familiar with the procedure for broadcasters, call public service directors of the stations and ask for guidelines.

Make your PSA brief. Usually just a few lines will be sufficient. Include a cover letter to the public service director and tell him who you are and something about your organization.

For a radio announcement, send a typed script. If you have multiple announcements, place each one on separate sheets. Lengths are 10 seconds for 10 words, 20 seconds with 20 words, and so on. Don't try to pre-record your announcement because the PSA director will have his own format.

For a TV announcement, follow the same procedure and include visuals. A color transparency will project a satisfactory image of your group. A photographer in your group could handle this.

Letters to the Editor

"Letters to the Editor" is one of the best read sections in a newspaper. You can be a "professional" letter writer and send letters to selected papers across the country. Small papers are more likely to print such letters. Multiple letters should be made to look personal, and whenever possible should refer to something of local interest in the paper's area. Robert Hohl has been very successful at this. He sends 50-100 copies of a letter expressing his viewpoint to papers across the country.

However, many editors will not print letters which appear to be part of a national campaign on an issue, unless the writer is a well known authority on the topic about which he is writing.

Large papers receive far more letters to the editor than they can publish. When a heavy run of mail is received on a controversial issue, an editor will choose "representative" letters for both sides. Editors also condense letters that are too long and correct obvious misspellings.

Your letter to the editor is more likely to be printed, if it is (1) well written, (2) no more than 300 words, (3) covers a topic of current interest, (4) is not defamatory, and (5) is signed, with your address and telephone number (home and work if possible) given at the end for verification.

Use a business letter format. Simply address "The Editor" or "Editorial Page Editor" at the location of the paper. Include a short catchy title if you wish, but don't be surprised if they change it.

You can find good examples in your own newspaper. Here's a letter by Laura Rogers, titled "Taping the Truth," that appeared in the May 10, 1990 issue of the St. Louis Post-Dispatch. Laura is the president of a coalition called National Parents and Childrens Association. One of their current concerns is the methods used in the prosecution of accused child abusers. Laura's letter, which appears in quotes under topic headings below, follows a format which may help you in preparing your letter to the editor.

1. Identify the Topic of Concern

A May 3 article [in the Post-Dispatch] says: 'Prosecutors from around the state helped to squelch a move [in the Missouri Legislature] Wednesday to require tape recordings of interviews with children who say they have been abused.

2. State the Facts

The unreported story is this. Prosecutors have trained professionals to tape record statements from children for years and have used them to get many convictions. But recently many of those taped inter-

views have also revealed that professionals are abusing children during the interviewing process.

3. Support the Facts

The tapes also reveal that doctors and other health professionals are coming into court with a bias that they are part of the prosecution team. Judges who see and hear these tapes have learned that the interviewing techniques produce unreliable results.

4. Present Your Argument

Prosecutors want it both ways. As long as prosecutors won cases with videotapes, prosecutors used videotapes. Now that their prosecution teams are caught abusing children during interviews, prosecutors want to squelch taping.

Since prosecutors seem to have a greater interest in winning their cases than getting to the truth, it may take the U.S. Supreme Court to tell them how to appropriately conduct interviews with children. An Idaho case now before the U.S. Supreme Court could significantly alter the way physicians interview children the state wants to use as witnesses. The position of the medical groups is that the health-care workers should be able to conduct interviews any way they want and still have them used as evidence. "That just isn't fair to those accused," said Rolfe Kehne, who argued the case before the U.S. Supreme Court in March.

5. Give a Positive Conclusion

Videotaping is a simple instrument to show the reliability of interviews with children, and it protects them from professional abuse.[14]

Laura's letter is not a tirade. It is a well-organized response to an effort to prevent the use in court trials of videotaped recordings of interviews with children alleged to have been sexually abused. Laura skillfully used facts to develop her case that such interviews should be used in court. (If you're interested in looking into the prosecution of alleged child abusers further, read <u>Guilty Until Proven Innocent</u> by Rev. Keith Barnhart, available from Hannibal Books.)

Write an Op-ed Article

An "op-ed" article is simply what the title suggests —opposite to the editorial page. You give your opinion on the subject of an editorial in a newspaper or magazine. Many radio and TV stations will also air a responsible answer to editorial positions taken by management.

This type of article is similar to a "letter to the editor," except that it is usually longer, more professionally written, and more fully developed. Some large papers pay for well-written op-ed articles.

It helps if you're known to the editor as a spokesperson for your group. Even so, it is advisable to send him a written query so he can discuss it with his staff before giving you the go ahead. When you do get the green light, ask several friends and trusted associates to write down some points which they think you could make. Take time to do a good article, but don't delay until the issue is out of the news.

Publicizing Your Big Event

Start the publicity bandwagon rolling weeks before the event.

- Eight months or more ahead: Decide on and secure your main speakers. Ask them for resumes for use in writing news releases.
- Six months ahead: Write a short news release, notifying community agencies of the event and date to get it on calendars printed by the Chamber of Commerce, the newspapers, and your city or area magazine.
- Four months ahead: Send news releases and other information to selected organizations who should be involved, including citizen groups, para-church organizations, churches, and others.
- One month ahead: Submit public service an-

nouncements to radio and TV stations. Contact local news media for feature stories. Send a longer news release than before along with other information to local media.

- Two weeks ahead: Do a direct mail blitz or organize your group to distribute flyers door-to door that announce the event. Place posters in stores and on church bulletin boards.
- One week after the event: Send thank you notes to all media and others who helped publicize the event.

You may not always be able to proceed according to the above time table. Sometimes you will have only a few weeks to make preparation.

As Winnebago County (Wisconsin) Chairman for the 1984 Reagan-Bush Presidential Campaign, I needed to stage a kick-off event. In order to draw the needed media and community support, I knew the program had to be both important and newsworthy. The national campaign headquarters suggested that the event feature nationally known people who could attract a wide variety of area residents.

After much discussion, the committee officers and I decided to ask Bart Starr, Coach of the Green Bay Packers, and three Packer players to participate. These four men were area celebrities and also known across the country. We held a press conference at the home of a local state senator and followed with the main program. The event was a complete success because it was newsworthy, timely, well-organized , and unique.

I later sent letters to all the media involved, expressing my appreciation for their professional and positive coverage.

Publicizing a Special Speaker

Here's an example which shows how you can use a variety of media to publicize your special speaker or event.

The Faith Baptist Church in Anchorage, Alaska hired Dr. James Hefley as their media consultant to publicize a coming week-long evangelistic crusade, to be led by Dr. Anis Shorrosh, a noted Palestinian evangelist. Upon learning that Baptists are a small minority in Anchorage, Dr. Hefley decided to build on Dr. Shorrosh's ethnic identity and the current high interest in the Middle East conflict.

Three weeks before coming to Anchorage, the consultant sent a press packet to the Anchorage media, obtaining addresses from broadcasting and newspaper directories available in his local library. The packet included a press release, a photo of the evangelist, a sheaf of feature articles written about Dr. Shorrosh in other cities, and catchy titles with one-paragraph summaries of Dr. Shorrosh's sermons which he planned to give at the church.

The consultant asked the church to display a banner above the main entrance to the sanctuary, four feet high, and twenty feet long, announcing in large, bold letters, THE PALESTINIAN IS COMING. He requested that the church insert the same announcement in small spot ads to appear daily in various sections of the two local newspapers during the week before the crusade began.

Dr. Hefley arrived six days before the first service was scheduled at the church. Volunteers drove him around to the newspapers and broadcast stations, where he contacted and got acquainted with key personnel (news directors at the stations and religion writers at the newspapers) and asked if they had received the media packet mailed two weeks before. He handed out additional media packets to those who could not remember receiving anything in the mail. He gave new press releases to all media and invited them to participate in a news conference at the airport an hour after Dr. Shorrosh's scheduled landing. The pastor had already reserved the room at the airport used for press conferences by important persons coming to Anchorage.

Several people told the consultant that they had heard a local, late-night TV host speculating on the identity of the Palestinian and why he was coming to Alaska. The host apparently had picked up on the teasers in the newspapers.

On the day of the speaker's scheduled arrival, the announcement was changed on the church banner and in the newspaper ads to read:

THE PALESTINIAN IS HERE AND SPEAKS TOMOR-
ROW AT FAITH BAPTIST CHURCH ON "WHAT KEPT
ME FROM BECOMING A TERRORIST."

The church youth prepared another banner, declaring,
ANCHORAGE WELCOMES THE PALESTINIAN. Dis-
playing the banner, they marched through the airport
lobby to await the arrival of the distinguished guest who
was due in at around one p.m. At the same time, local
media began arriving for the press conference.

To everyone's dismay, "The Palestinian's" plane was
several hours late in arriving because of a snow storm at
an intermediate stop in Minneapolis. Dr. Hefley expressed
his regrets to the media and promised to bring the visitor,
if he arrived in time, to the TV stations for an appearance
on the six o'clock evening news.

When Dr. Shorrosh's plane finally landed at about five
p.m. the young people from the church were still there, but
the media had long since departed. Seeking to make the
most of the situation, the consultant took the evangelist
to two TV stations where he was interviewed on the
nightly news.

The next day "The Palestinian" was welcomed by a
record crowd at the church. During the week almost 100
persons made professions of faith in Christ during the
services, breaking another church record for an evangelistic crusade. The church also received the largest offering
ever received since its founding.

The newspapers ran long feature stories on the guest
preacher. When the crusade ended, the pastor reported
that Baptists in Alaska had received more publicity about
the event than anything else presented in the past 25
years in the state.

Not until returning home to Tennessee did the consultant, Dr. Hefley, learn that the Anchorage media had
clashed several months before with several local Baptist
ministers over a moral issue in the mayoralty election. "I
read some of the unfriendly stories in newspapers sent to
me by a media friend in Anchorage," Dr. Hefley told me.
"It was a good thing I didn't know about this until after
the media campaign for the evangelistic meeting. If I had,
I probably would have gone to Alaska expecting to be

received poorly by the media. As it happened, I went there expecting the media to be helpful, and they were."

How to Prepare for a TV Interview

If you are the chairman of an important coalition or civic event in your community you will likely be called upon to represent that group on television. If you are well known in your city as an advocate of a particular position in a controversy, you could get a call at any time to represent that position.

In the 1988 Presidential campaign, I was notified one and a half hours ahead of time to appear live on the six p.m. news in a city one hour and fifteen minutes away. The station manager gave me three possible questions the interviewer might ask. I felt confident I could answer any one or all of them.

I quickly changed into clothes which would present a clean, crisp appearance, making it a point to avoid strong colors and flashy jewelry. I wanted my message to get attention, not me. On the way to the station I rehearsed answers in my mind, while also keeping an eye on the road, of course. I walked into the studio less than two minutes before air time. The station manager quickly gave me the format for the interview, stuck an ear plug in my ear, and directed my attention to the interviewer on the overhead TV. The interview progressed satisfactorily.

Here are ten suggestions—some of which I picked up from author Lee Roddy—which I've found helpful in preparing for an interview on TV. They're also good to keep in mind when being interviewed by anyone else, including a newspaper reporter.

- Be well groomed—hair combed, light makeup, nails trimmed; face freshly shaved if you're a man. If you're old enough to remember the Nixon-Kennedy presidential debates in 1960, you may remember Nixon's legendary "five o'clock shadow." According to observers, Nixon "walked all over Kennedy" on content, but lost on appearance.
- Dress neatly and in a contemporary style. Avoid anything loud or unusual which will detract from

your message.

- Try to know ahead of time what questions will be asked. Ask the manager if they want brief statements or detailed summaries.
- As much as possible, become familiar with the interviewer's style, verbal cues, format, and types of questions asked.
- Position yourself in the chair before the camera light comes on. Watch your body language. Let your voice tone, facial expressions, and other mannerisms show confidence and conviction.
- Stick to the issue and don't ramble. If you're a neophyte, rehearse answers to possible questions with a friend who will play "devil's advocate." Political candidates do this routinely.
- Before you go on camera, know how you will answer the anticipated questions. For example, if you're being interviewed about pro-life legislation before your state legislature, you might be asked, "Would you be in favor of punishing a woman for getting an abortion?" You might answer, "No woman before 1973 was ever prosecuted under the abortion statutes. Criminal action was taken against the doctor. Women are really co-victims in an abortion. Pro-life people want to ease suffering."
Here's another example: "If abortion is outlawed, won't thousands of women die at the hands of back alley butchers?" Possible answer: "The Centers for Disease Control (CDC) figures show otherwise. In 1972, the year before Roe v. Wade, only 39 women were known to have died from illegal abortions. Ten years later the number who died from legal abortions was 24. Abortion is still a dangerous procedure."[75]
- Smile and keep your chin up, both figuratively and literally. When the interviewer cites something negative about you or your organization, keep smiling.
- Listen carefully to what the interviewer is saying and use only the facts when responding. I force everything else from my mind so that I'm able to

concentrate on my choice of words and the manner in which I speak.

- Keep your eye on the interviewer, and speak calmly. Correct mistakes with a smile without berating the interviewer or an opponent who may be appearing on camera with you.
- Thank the station manager or news director for having you on. Say a good word to the interviewer too, even if he did make a nasty insinuation.

How to Hold a Press Conference

If your group brings a VIP to town, wishes to propose a solution to a critical problem, or one of your members decides to run for Congress, you may wish to call a press conference. How do you determine if your story is "newsworthy?" Ask yourself what other big story will you be competing with at the time? How will your "news" look on TV? Will it be of high interest to a variety of people? If the answers to these questions are "yes," the next step is to plan the press conference. The following suggestions may be of help:

- Before setting the date and time of your press conference, check with local media to see if there would be a conflict with some other major event. United Press International and the Associated Press will have a day book listing upcoming events of news significance.
- Monday through Thursday are usually the best days. Avoid the lunch hour, but don't schedule later than two p.m., so your story can be prepared for the evening TV news. On Friday, the media will be wrapping up their week's work and even if some attend your conference, the news is likely to die over the weekend. Saturday and Sunday are out because publishers and broadcasters don't like to pay overtime. Distribute announcements to the media two or three weeks ahead if possible, then make reminder calls 24 hours in advance. Contact editors, station news directors, and specific media persons who specialize in the topic to be addressed at the press conference.

- Hold the press conference at a convenient place for the media to attend. A downtown hotel will rent a conference room for this purpose and also provide coffee, juice, and pastries for refreshments. Be sure and reserve the room far enough ahead of time. If you think this is too expensive, look for a public facility.
- Have press kits ready to hand out before the conference begins. A kit should include a press release geared to the topic of the press conference, biographies, black and white photos of the personalities appearing, a statement of your organization's purpose and goals, a list of key issues which your group is working on, and press clippings of previous stories about the personalities and your group.
- The chairman of the sponsoring group should preside and serve as moderator at a press conference held for a visiting dignitary. Have a table set up on which press packets can be placed and reporters can lay their tape recorders. The personality should speak from a lectern just behind the table. Use a microphone and check out sound equipment before the meeting begins if over 50 people are present.
- Welcome the media. Read a short prepared statement about the reason for the conference. Then introduce the personality who may wish to make an opening statement before receiving questions.
- Occasionally you may have a panel to answer questions. Be sure that each panel member is introduced properly and has a microphone before him. Panel members should speak from a sitting position.
- In a small room, the questions can be informally directed to the personality, persons on the panel, or whoever is announcing the big news. In a large room, the person presiding should repeat each question so all can hear, then let the personality answer.
- Do not allow two or three aggressive reporters monopolize the conference. Give every member of the media present a chance to ask a question, then allow follow-ups. Also, in the case of a panel, see that each

panel member participates. You can do this by
directing general questions to different persons on
the panel.

- Be knowledgeable of press terminology. If you want
to make a statement, but don't want it printed or
broadcast, be sure to tell the reporters, "This is off
the record," or "this is background." When you say
"no comment" to a reporter, it's like saying, "I'm lying
and I can't tell you." It's best to explain why you don't
want to comment.

- After a designated time for asking questions—usually no longer than 45 minutes—the distinguished
visitor, chairman of the group, or a panel member
should be invited to give a brief wrap-up statement.
Then, before formal dismissal, invite interested
media to make appointments for personal interviews. Also after dismissal, allow photographers to
take any additional pictures they may need.

- Tape record the entire press conference. The tape
may be useful in later refuting a damaging misquote.

- Hand deliver press kits to media people who could
not attend.

I'm sure I haven't covered everything about using the
media to reach the largest possible audience. Ask friends
in the media for tips on more effective media relations.
Check out a library book or take a course at the university
on public relations. Plan your work and work your plan. If
you are to reach your goal, people must know what you are
attempting to do and why. Use media—personal, supportive, and public—to spread your message.

Declared Wendell Phillips, a well-known 19th century
American reformer and orator: "Let me make the
newspapers, and I care not what is preached in the pulpit
or what is enacted in Congress."

Napoleon feared "four opposing newspapers" more
"than a thousand bayonets."[76] What would Phillips
and Napoleon say about the media today?

Yes, people in the media are often biased and sometimes
anti-Christian. Yes, they often do not understand issues
from the Judeo-Christian perspective. But do not let these

difficulties stand in your way of using the media and the technology of spreading information to inform the citizenry about what must be done to really change America for the better. Learn how the media works and turn perceived disadvantages into advantages.

"We do not have a personal gospel and a social gospel. There is one Gospel, and one Gospel only, and that Gospel is the Gospel of God. This indivisible message from God has its individual application and its social application. It has the power to redeem the individual and also the power to redeem the social order."
Jesse M. Bader

Chapter 13

Involving the Church

Without Christianity and the Bible, there would never have been "a land of the free and home of the brave." All of the institutions which made this nation great are rooted in Biblical foundations. The Supreme Court has declared America to be "a Christian nation" by heritage.

James Madison, the chief architect of our Constitution, said, "We have staked the whole of all our political institutions . . . upon the capacity of each and all of us to govern ourselves, to control ourselves, to sustain ourselves according to the Ten Commandments of God."

This was no secret to the generation that preceded us. The "old" public school histories made it plain that Christians and the church built and sustained American society. Now—thanks to decades of brainwashing by zealous secularists—most people think America is only a pluralistic society, in which Christianity is only one part. Try asking a high school senior if he can quote even one line from the Mayflower Compact.

The church (I am speaking generically here) started slipping in influence in the first decades of this century when our educational system began sliding into secularism. Today God and Christian symbols have been virtually banished from public schools.

The Perils of Pluralism

A directive sent to principals in the Corpus Christi, Texas School District declares: "The legal staff strongly recommends the deletion of sectarian music from Christmas programs such as 'Away in a Manger,' 'Silent Night,' etc. Their best advice is to keep the music as 'heathen' as possible by using selections such as 'Jingle Bells,' 'Rudolph the Red-Nosed Reindeer,' 'Feliz Navidad,' etc."[77]

An old college buddy was telling me about her public school history class: "My students really enjoyed learning about our pluralistic society."

"Wait a minute, Kathy," I broke in. "Our what society?"

"Pluralistic—oh, here we go again, Darylann."

"Kathy, this is supposed to be a Christian nation. At least it was founded by Christian people who had that intent."

"Darylann, that's just your right-wing view. Look at our textbooks. They don't talk about a Christian nation. It's pluralism that has made America great."

It was no use to argue with Kathy, for she has been brainwashed by the shapers of secular thought.

Sadly, many Christians have the same opinion. Talk to them about politics and civic action and they say, "That's not what the church is for."

It's a good thing that our Christians forefathers didn't think this way.

It is not that the church in America is small in numbers. A 1990 Gallup Poll discovered that 69 percent of all Americans—172 million—profess affiliation with a religious denomination. Think what would happen if only one tenth of these professing believers should set to work to restore the ideals which we have lost.

Why Did Christians Pull Out of the Civic Arena?

Well, it didn't happen overnight. Church historians trace the beginning to a revival of pietism, sparked by a German immigrant named Philip Jakob Spener. Mr.

Spener never said that Christians should get out of politics. He called for a revival of piety. He said that spirituality should be at the center of the church. Nothing wrong with that. What happened was that Bible-believing Christians began dividing their world into the sacred and the secular, and saying that the church should stay out of the secular area. At the same time, church liberals began trying to change the world by political action, while neglecting Biblical authority and the spiritual life.

Both approaches proved inadequate.

Liberals lost their spiritual power base by moving away from the authority of Scripture and failing to proclaim the necessity of a personal relationship with God through Jesus Christ. Conservative evangelicals abandoned society and politics to the religious liberals and secularists who worked for the de-Christianization of America.

One branch of the evangelicals said the world is getting worse and worse and Jesus is coming back soon. Politics and everything else in secular society is corrupt and cannot be reformed, they reasoned. So let's keep our prophecy charts up to date and keep speculating on when Christ will return.

Another branch said that the church should devote all its outreach to evangelizing. If we win enough people to Christ, we will change society, they believed.

These folks were sincere. But by pulling out of the citizen arena, they left a tremendous spiritual vacuum in education, the media, government, and everything else outside the four walls of the church.

Thankfully these attitudes began to change in the late 1960's when it became obvious that militant secularists were out to take over society. When Bible believing Christians did break out of their chambers, the secularists were ready with a quick rejoinder: "You're violating the separation of church and state." That was often all it took to send many Christians running back to their closets.

The Great "Separation" Myth

Then and now many Christians think the phrase "separation of church and state" is in the Constitution. It is not. It is in Article 52 of the Constitution of the Soviet

Union.

Here's how the phrase "separation of church and state" originated. Fifteen years after the U.S. Constitution was written, Thomas Jefferson used it in a letter to the Danbury Baptist Association in Connecticut. The Danbury Baptists were worried that the Congregational Church would become the official church in that state. Jefferson was assuring them that the First Amendment placed a wall of separation between a church denomination and the state. Jefferson's Second Inaugural Address shows that he meant that the wall was to protect the church from the federal government, not the other way around. The wall of separation was to guarantee freedom of religion, not freedom from religion. Look at the First Amendment and you'll see what the Constitution really says:

> *Congress shall make no law respecting an establishment of religion, or prohibiting the free exercise thereof; or abridging the freedom of speech, or of the press; or the right of the people peaceably to assemble, and to petition the Government for a redress of grievances.*

That's all it says.

Obviously, there are differences in what individuals and the church as a corporate body can do in political activities. The church is not a human structure like a political, social, or economic body, although it has members from many human organizations and nations. It is the "fellowship of saints" (1 Peter 2:9 KJV), the "building" of which Jesus is the chief corner-stone or foundation, "an habitation of God through the Spirit." (Ephesians 2:20 KJV).As the people of Christ, the church is commanded (1) to proclaim the Gospel and make disciples in every nation (Matthew 28:18-20), and (2) teach and encourage Christians to apply Biblical truth to every relationship of life. (Ephesians 4:12-16) That includes our responsibilities as citizens, as individuals, and as part of the church body.

What a Minister Can Do

An individual church member can do anything in

politics that any other citizen can do: run for office, endorse candidates, contribute funds, work in a political campaign.

So can a minister, when he is acting on his own. However, he should be respectful of the affiliations of his church members and not use his office to favor one political party or one candidate (except in unusual cases) over another. A minister must decide where these limits lie and which roles are most appropriate. A minister, for example, might choose to "run" for the school board, but not to serve as a campaign manager for a partisan political candidate.

As the leader of a local church, a minister can, from the pulpit, encourage members to vote and be active in the political party of their choice. He can preach on moral righteousness and show how God's laws can be applied in human relations and society. He can take stands on moral issues and assist in the establishment of a moral concerns group within the church. He can instruct members to respect and obey the law (except when in conflict with the express will of God) and pay tax obligations to civil authorities (Romans 13:1-7).

What a Church Can and Cannot Do

A church, as a corporate, non-profit organization, must play a somewhat different role. The church's tax-exempt status may be lost by improper involvement in political affairs. By federal law, a church cannot directly or indirectly participate in any political campaign, either for or in opposition to a candidate. A church body cannot endorse a candidate for office by action of the church body or any official group in the church. Nor can the church treasurer give church funds to political parties or candidates.

Here are some things that a church can do:

- Engage in nonpartisan voter registration and voter education as long as the church does not officially endorse a political party.
- Invite candidates from all parties to submit written answers to questions on issues. How or if the candidates respond is up to them. This information can be given to church members along with a list of all the candidates.

- Hold a forum to hear the views from all candidates on issues that affect the church members. The Federal Election Commission advises that such forums are the only way a tax exempt organization, classified as a church, can hold a political debate.
- Recognize a candidate in a service. However, it is illegal for a candidate to address a church service in pursuit of funds for his campaign, although this has been done in many black churches.
- Dispense information about moral concerns in the community. It is also sometimes possible for a church to join a coalition of other churches and citizen groups who are contending for a moral issue. A church should exercise care in becoming involved in voter referendums. It is always best to have an attorney check local and state ordinances before becoming involved in an electoral issue which some define as "political." For example, a group of Baptist churches in Jackson, TN were threatened with revocation of their state tax exemption after they opposed a local referendum on the sale of alcohol.

The Persecution of the Church

We in the church must be ever alert to encroachments upon our rights under the Constitution. We need to be especially watchful of so-called civil rights legislation which could make churches hire homosexuals, people with AIDS, alcoholics, or even atheists. The Civil Rights Restoration Act of 1988 requires that any institution using any direct or indirect federal aid not discriminate in employment. The Act does permit a church or religious organization to apply for a religious tenets' exemption from the legislation. But this is like being required to prove your innocence after being declared guilty. Under this Act Catholic Georgetown University was ordered by a judge to provide funds and a meeting place for a club of homosexual students. And a Mississippi federal district judge ordered a local Salvation Army unit to rehire a "witch" who had been fired for using the Army's copy machine to reproduce witchcraft materials.

We must not be caught napping. There are powerful

forces in America seeking to drive the church out of public
life. A suit by pro-abortion groups, which included some
rabbis and liberal Protestant ministers, contended that
the Catholic Church had violated Internal Revenue Service rules by lobbying against legalized abortion and contributing to candidates who opposed abortion. The suit
contended that the IRS had, by failing to cancel tax exemption status, "granted the church the equivalent of a
cash subsidy for partisan political activity."

Some of the groups filing this suit held tax-exempt
status themselves. Their lawyers said the groups had
refrained from lobbying and making political contribu-
tions, thus suffering a competitive disadvantage in the
national struggle over abortion.

The Second U.S. Circuit Court of Appeals, by a 2-1 vote,
ruled against the plaintiffs in September, 1989. The court
majority said the pro-choice groups lacked standing because they were "spectators" who were admittedly not
engaged in the alleged political activity.

The suit was appealed to the Supreme Court which, in
1990, let stand the ruling of the lower court. The Supreme
Court had previously voted 8-1 to free the Catholic Church
from having to pay $100,000 a day in court fines for
withholding documents sought by the groups favoring
legalized abortion.[78]

Homosexual activists, radical feminists, and groups
trying to preserve legalized abortion continue to vigorous-
ly oppose churches and ministers who take their stands
against sinful abominations and threats to the survival of
America.

John Cardinal O'Connor was just beginning his sermon
at St. Patrick's Cathedral in New York on a Sunday in
December, 1989, when 40 homosexual activists began
heckling and screaming from the pews.

"O'Connor, you're a murderer!" yelled one. Another
pretended to come forward for communion. He snatched
the wafer, crushed it between his fingers, and threw it on
the floor. Others chained themselves to pews and sprawled
in the aisles, screaming obscenities and blocking wor-
shipers. New York Post columnist Ray Kerrison, watching
from the pews, wrote:

*"In all my life, I have never witnessed a spectacle quite
like that which shook St. Patrick's Cathedral . . . when
radical homosexuals turned a celebration of the Holy
Eucharist into a screaming babble of sacrilege by standing in the pews, shouting and waving their fists, tossing
shredded paper and condoms into the air, and forcing
squads of cops lining the aisles to arrest them."*

Outside, almost 5000 homosexuals and feminists carried on an even noisier protest. They carried signs that
said, "Keep your rosaries off my ovaries," "Eternal life to
Cardinal O'Connor NOW!" The demonstrators carried
with them a 20-foot long balloon which they called "Cardinal O'Condom."

Evangelical churches and ministers, courageous enough
to stand against open sin and sacrilege, are feeling the
heat too. Take what recently happened in the little town
of Mora, Minnesota.

The trouble began after Assembly of God pastor David
Squire and other concerned parents objected to an AIDS
and sex education curriculum in the public schools which
their children attended. Their specific concern was a play
called "Amazing Grace" which included a brief video
documentary of an AIDS victim and portrayed the
homosexual lifestyle as normal and acceptable.

Pastor Squire, himself the parent of a high school senior,
and the parents' group, Concerned Parents for Abstinence,
protested the play and the curriculum before the school
board just before the school year ended. The board appointed a task force to investigate their charges.

While the minister was away on vacation, his deacons
called to warn him that a thousand radical homosexuals
and lesbians planned to picket the church. Only 170
showed up, but police stood by to prevent a riot. The
picketers passed out leaflets that declared, "David Squire
Oppresses," and called for "separation of church and state"
in the community. They demanded that the pastor
apologize for "his contribution to the AIDS crisis through
his ignorance, fear, and intolerance of sexual diversity."
They asked that alternatives to sexual abstinence be ex-
plicitly taught in schools.

Pastor Squire refused to back down. "Am I to stop condemning sin as sin?" he asked. "That seems to have become an obsolete word in our society, but God has not changed. I would have been remiss if I hadn't spoken out. I could just as well have spoken about gossip, lying, cheating, adultery, drunkenness or drug abuse."

The invasion of little Mora by militant gays appeared to do their cause more harm than good. In the fall, following the controversy, Concerned Parents for Abstinence succeeded in electing a Christian activist to the school board. "I think we put the 'public' back in public education," Pastor Squire said. "We've encouraged people to be active in the school because there are things being taught that Christian people would not tolerate or appreciate."[79]

How to Start a Moral Concerns Group in Your Church

Every church needs an on-going moral concerns group to research and keep members aware of needs in the community, state, and nation. The structure and number of people involved will depend on the membership of the local body. Here are some ideas for organizing a group:

Start by meeting with a few people you know are already interested. Invite the pastor and the chairman of the deacons to participate in the discussion of how a moral concerns group can be established. Have someone keep minutes on the discussion. At this first meeting, ask for volunteers to serve on a temporary executive committee. This leadership could serve in an ad hoc capacity until the idea has been accepted by the church.

The number of persons in the group is not nearly as important as the exercise of their talents and commitment. The chairperson is responsible for overseeing the entire operation. He is the liaison with the church and its officers. He should keep the pastor and deacons informed of activities of the group.

The group will also need a secretary, treasurer, and a number of task forces or committees.

The secretary writes up the minutes, notifies members of scheduled meetings, and handles all group correspondence.

The treasurer keeps a record of expenses and arranges for payment of authorized bills. The group can be financed by a budget allotment from the general church treasury, designated gifts, or by special fund-raising events.

The legislative committee keeps in touch with local officials, state representatives and Congressmen, and reports back to the group. This committee informs the group when a political leader changes his stance on abortion, pornography, or some other moral issues of concern.

The legislative committee should stay in touch with representatives on upcoming legislation of interest to the church. Committee members should ask the legislators for personal prayer requests and place a picture of each lawmaker on the group's prayer bulletin board. They should also stay in contact with denominational lobbyists in the state capitol and in Washington to receive information and let them know where the local church stands.

The public relations committee should prepare and mail a monthly newsletter to church members. The newsletter will keep everyone up to date on findings of the legislative committee. This mailing can be included with the church newsletter. This sub-group can teach the congregation how to write effective letters to newspapers and elected officials.

The educational committee should plan and offer an on-going program of studies on current moral issues and Christian citizenship. They should also invite political candidates to speak to the group from time to time. They should develop an information center or bulletin board where a large number of people pass. Besides prayer concerns, the display should include updates on current issues, newsletter information, newspaper clippings, city news, letters from elected officials, announcements of helpful books which can be checked out from the church or public library, and the names, addresses, and phone numbers of the officers and committee chairs of the group. Under the bulletin board or next to the display have a small table for literature, brochures, a suggestion box, and sign-up cards for volunteer jobs.

The voting committee should keep the entire church

membership informed on issues and candidates before every election. Sixty days before the election they should provide registration cards and information on registering to all eligible voters, explain the voting districts, and pinpoint the voting places on precinct maps.

They can ask the pastor to make an announcement in the Sunday service before election day and explain the process of voting.

This committee can also work with other groups in promoting a community wide voter registration drive. In recent national elections little more than 50 percent of the eligible voters made it to the polls. The turnout of eligible Christian voters is no better than the average. The voting committee should enlist a sufficient number of volunteers to call every church member of voting age on the day of the election. Remind them to vote. Offer to provide a ride to the polls and to make available baby sitting service. Tell those who are indifferent that voting is a part of Christian stewardship. Poll workers in a small town in northeastern Wisconsin had one man paged three times at a local high school football game before he consented to go vote at halftime.

In all of this, the voting committee must not promote one candidate above another. If the group has educated the church members on the positions of the candidates, they will vote the right way. The important thing now is to see that they vote.

Challenging Liberal Church Lobbyists

To this point, we have considered what the members, minister, and the body of a local church can do in citizenship responsibilities and moral concerns. Your church should also consider its affiliate responsibilities as a member of a denomination or some other fellowship.

Your church is probably already sending a certain amount or a percentage of budget money to denominational headquarters. These funds are apportioned by a denominational committee to foreign missions, home missions, seminaries, public affairs, etc. The public affairs department may have an office in Washington from which staff members lobby government officials on legislation

and regulations which affect local churches and relationships between church and state. These lobbyists claim to
represent their respective denominations. They know that
a congressman, for example, from a district with a large
Methodist population will pay special attention to what a
United Methodist lobbyist says about pending legislation.

The bad news for conservative Christians in the mainline denominations is that their religious lobbyists tend to
support legalized abortion and other liberal programs
which many constituents do not favor.

The good news is that there are conservative renewal
organizations within every one of these denominations
calling for lobbyist accountability to their supporters.

One of the most effective of these renewal organizations
is the United Methodist "Good News" group which was
started by Rev. Charles Keysor in the office of his church
in Elgin, IL. Good News now publishes books and also a
magazine by that name, holds conferences, and educates
fellow United Methodists on issues within their own
church. The Good News people are not trying to split their
denomination. They are calling for theological and moral
renewal within their church structures and for better
representation before government.

The mainline denominations have lost hundreds of
thousands of members during the past quarter-century.
United Methodists alone dropped one half in Sunday
School enrollment. The renewal groups blame the membership losses to liberal political activism and the depar-
ture from Biblical authority by many church leaders.

Largely because of the Good News group, the highest
official body of the United Methodist Church has rejected
ordination of avowed, practicing homosexuals. But the
issue is not dead. An official committee is studying the
issue and is due to report to the United Methodist General
Conference in 1992. James Robb, senior editor of the Good
News magazine, says that less than a fourth of the 24
committee members oppose the ordination of
homosexuals.

Robb recently stirred an uprising among Methodist
pro-life people by reporting close Washington ties between
their denominational staff people and the Religious Coali-

tion for Abortion Rights (RCAR) which supports Roe v. Wade and favors legalized abortion during the first trimester of pregnancy for any and all reasons. Robb reported that for the first eight years of its existence, RCAR and the United Methodist Board of Church and Society were virtually one and the same. Robb noted that the RCAR group was still meeting in a United Methodist-owned building and that an executive staff member of the Women's Division of his denomination was serving as president of RCAR.

Members of the Evangelical Lutheran Church of America have also formed a coalition for "disenchanted segments" of the church. The coalition serves as an umbrella organization for conservative Evangelical Lutheran Church groups across the country who are worried about trends within the denomination. The groups are especially concerned about the ordination of homosexuals into the Lutheran ministry.

Should Gays Be Ordained?

Every major denomination has one or more militant homosexual groups lobbying for the acceptance of homosexual ministers and the acceptance of homosexuality as a "normal" life style. The president of the gay and lesbian organization in the Episcopal Church says an average of five self-avowed, non-celibate homosexuals and lesbians have been ordained every year in that church since 1977. This man claims that before 1977, "hundreds" of practicing homosexuals were ordained who were not "out of the closet" at the time they were set apart for the ministry.[80]

Whether true or not, the ordination of homosexuals is not approved of by most Episcopalians. A survey of more than 100,000 found 89 percent of them opposing ordination of avowed, practicing homosexuals and 88 percent opposing the "blessing" of homosexual "unions" by clergy. The survey was reported in February, 1990 by Rev. Ted Nelson, chairman of Episcopalians United for Revelation, Renewal, and Reformation.

The issue of homosexual ordination is causing great consternation in this denomination. A visiting black bishop from Kenya was recently "disinvited" from speaking in an Episcopal Church in San Francisco because he planned to speak out against homosexuality. Bishop Alexander Muge noted that his invitation to speak was canceled after "I pointed out" to the ministerial staff "that the decline of the [Episcopal] Church in the USA is due to the secularization of the gospel and the lack of self discipline among the clergy in the church; those who should set a good example but fail to. I further pointed out," he notes, "that homosexuals and lesbians have taken over the [Episcopal] church leadership in the USA and there is no way God is going to bless this church with growth."[81]

Baptist Battles

Denominational lobbyists have a powerful influence both in Washington and in their denominations. The Baptist Joint Committee on Public Affairs (BJCPA) pushed through a resolution at the 1964 Southern Baptist Convention indirectly endorsing the landmark Supreme Court decisions outlawing school-sponsored prayer and Bible reading in public schools. Justice Arthur Goldberg later admitted that the BJCPA-sponsored SBC resolution kept the high court from being impeached after the tumultuous outcry following the precedent-setting rulings.

The BJCPA represents nine Baptist bodies. Southern Baptists have been the largest financial supporter, giving about 90 percent of the organization's budget during recent years, while holding only a third of the votes in the group. Southern Baptist conservatives oppose this disparity in funding and alignment of the BJCPA with causes favored by the American Civil Liberties Union, Norman Lear's People for the American Way (PAW), and Americans United for Church and State. The Executive Director of the BJCPA resigned from the PAW board after pressure was applied by conservative Southern Baptist pastors and laymen.

What can grassroots church members do about lobbying activities of denominational employees with whom they cannot agree?

• The local church's moral concerns group can request

reports on the positions and actions of these lobbyists, and make this information known to the
church.
- With authorization from the local church, the moral
concerns group can call press conferences and
present their concerns at denominational meetings.
- They can network with moral concerns groups in
other churches of their denomination, and form a
united front for making the denominational public
affairs office in Washington more responsible to
supporters.

Church Ministries To Meet Special Needs

Jesus commanded Christians to reach out to people with
special needs. "Inasmuch as you have done it unto one of
the least of these, my brethren, you have done it unto me."
(Matthew 25:40, KJV)

Across the land, many churches are doing just that—
backing up their preaching with deeds of mercy. The
Roswell Street Baptist Church in Marietta,GA, is an outstanding example. This conservative, Bible-teaching
church provides:

- A crisis pregnancy center which has aided 5,000
women, who have given birth to 2,000 babies who
otherwise might have been aborted.
- A home for unwed mothers.
- A Christian counseling service for individuals and
families.
- A substance-abuse program which provides help for
drug and alcohol abusers.
- Co-dependency classes which aid family members of
substance abusers.
- A summer literacy program in which elementary-
age children receive remedial services in reading.
- Twenty thousand dollars a year to feed, clothe, and
shelter needy people.
- Efforts to improve race relations which include joint
worship services with black congregations.
- A 10,000-watt radio station which can reach three
million people with moral and spiritual instruction.

The church is now negotiating to buy a low-power TV station that could reach 1.5 million people in the Atlanta area.
• An annual writers conference for ministers and laity.

Pastor Nelson Price has made a special effort to develop friendships and pray with political leaders on both sides of the aisle. He preached the inauguration sermon for President Jimmy Carter. But it was by serving on Georgia's Board of Human Resources that he became awakened to the challenge of church minstries to special community needs.

The Greatest Power of the Church

In this book, we have been primarily concerned with the challenge for Christians to become involved in politics and citizen affairs. We have seen how the conscience of America has been turned away from the great Biblical values on which our country was founded and followed for many decades.

One reason for this is that many Christians, commanded to be "light" and "salt" in society, have dropped out of citizen responsibilities. A more foundational reason is that many of our churches have lost their power. They are more concerned about pomp, beautiful buildings, and rank in the community than prophetically proclaiming the Word of God and praying for revival.

Moral and ethical decay in America runs much deeper than most of us suppose. At root, this decay is a rebellion of wrong against eternal right, putting authority above divine law. These roots of rebellion and sin, in every human heart, cannot be fully addressed by laws and political action. If our ultimate aim is to make men good, the really big question is: how do we make them good?

Daniel Webster wrote, "Whatever makes men good Christians, makes them good citizens." Who can disagree?

In the final analysis, real and lasting goodness results only when an individual repents of sin, accepts the love and forgiveness provided by Christ's sacrifice on the cross, and develops a mature Christian life by a daily walk with

God.

We cannot legislate enduring change in the thoughts
and attitudes of individuals. However, if enough Christians with spiritual stature will begin living by Biblical
standards and assume leadership in society, then we can
rebuild the foundations of the representative and responsible government that made America great.

The influence and image of Christians has been hurt
more than we will probably ever know by moral compromise. The television ministry scandals are only the "tip
of the iceberg" of the unholy living that permeates
American Christianity. Unfortunately, some of those who
claim to believe the Bible the most are guilty of practicing
God's Word the least.

It is the church that must call us back to the disciplines
of prayer and repentance that is necessary for revival, as
laid down in the Bible almost 3,000 years ago: "If my
people, which are called by my name, shall humble themselves, and pray, and seek my face, and turn from their
wicked ways; then will I hear from heaven, and will forgive
their sin, and will heal their land." (2 Chronicles 7:14 KJV)

Our prayer for revival must be matched by the discipline
of self-denial, which in my judgment includes fasting. The
history of revivals from Biblical times until now shows
that spiritual power comes by both fasting and prayer.

Revival and the American Revolution

Go with me back to the mid-18th century when the
churches in the colonies were filled with unconverted
"Halfway members" who had been accepted into
"covenant" church membership on the basis of doing certain spiritual duties. These "means" were supposed to
prepare them for regeneration by the Holy Spirit.

The greatest preacher of that time, Jonathan Edwards,
denounced the "Halfway Covenant" and called for personal faith and repentance from sin. "None of our own
excellency, virtue, or righteousness," he declared, "is the
ground of our being received from a state of condemnation
into a state of acceptance in God's sight, but only Jesus
Christ, and His righteousness, and worthiness, received
by faith."

The revival, under Edwards, began in Northhampton, Massachusetts. Soon, in Edwards' words, "There was scarcely a single person in the town, either old or young, left unconcerned about the great things of the eternal world."[82]

The great Methodist evangelist George Whitefield came from England to assist Edwards and other colonial ministers in the revival effort. American Christians became united as never before. Meetings were filled with sobs as thousands upon thousands of people repented of their sins and claimed Christ as their Savior. An estimated one-sixth of the population of New England was converted and received into the churches.

The "Great Awakening" purified the American people for the coming revolution. The revival gave the people the moral courage to fight for freedom and to establish a new nation "under God, indivisible, with liberty and justice for all."

This revival did not lead believers to isolate themselves in church buildings. Led by the Spirit of God, they moved out into society to build the foundations of a purified nation.

The "Awakening" We Need

Let us not fall into the humanistic trap of thinking that more laws and skilled "Christian" politicians alone can change America. Only another "great awakening," followed by righteous living and moral reform can do that.

Janet Parshall, National Board Member for Concerned Women for America of Wisconsin, puts this well: "We must be persistent and committed in the battle for America. At stake is nothing less than the hearts and minds of our children, nothing less than the ability of our nation's workforce to compete in the future world economy, nothing less than the competence of our future citizens to run the great engines of American democracy. For the sake of our children and our grandchildren, let us join the battle today."

So may it be, Lord. So may it be.

FOOTNOTES

[1] Speech to National Religious Broadcasters' convention, Washington, D.C., February, 1983.

[2] Mel and Norma Gabler: What Are They Teaching Our Children? Victor Books, Wheaton, Illinois, 1985, p. 150.

[3] Dr. Block's Illustrated Human Sexuality Book for Kids, PREP Publishing Co., 1979, pp. 206-208.

[4] Masculinity and Femininity, Instructor's Guide, Houghton Mifflin Co., New York, N.Y., 1971, p. 12.

[5] George W. Cornell: "Gallup Poll Shows Americans Oppose Drugs, Free Sex . . . ," Hannibal Courier-Post, Hannibal, MO, June 24, 1989.)

[6] James C. Hefley: America: One Nation Under God, Victor Books, Wheaton, IL, 1976, p. 12.

[7] Ibid, p. 15.

[8] Ibid, p. 18.

[9] Quoted from Life's Answer Magazine, Box 18489, Ft. Worth, TX 76118.

[10] One Nation Under God, op. cit., p. 21.

[11] Rochunga Pudaite: The Greatest Book Ever Written, Hannibal Books, Hannibal, MO, 1989, p. 133.

[12] America: One Nation Under God, Op. cit. p. 11

[13] Ibid, p. 80.

[14] Psychology for You, Oxford Book Company, New York, N.Y., 1973, p. 191.

[15] Unfinished Journey: A World History, Houghton Mifflin Company, New York, N.Y., 1983, pp. 720-721.

[16] Life and Health, Random House, Third Edition, New

York, N.Y.,1980, p. 161, figure 9.4.

[17]Cited in The Impact of Federal Involvement on Public Education," Maryland Federation of Republican Women's Study Guide, 1976, pp. 6-7.

[18]Macmillan Gateway English, Teacher's Manual, The Macmillan Company, New York, NY, 1970, p. 28.

[19]Reported from the April, 1989 issue of the Stanford Review by Focus on the Family magazine, August, 1989, p. 5.

[20]Charles Shofstahl: "Professor Persecuted for His Faith," Christian Inquirer, February, 1985, p. 26.

[21]"College Daze, St. Louis Post-Dispatch, October 9, 1989, pp. 1, 7.

[22]"Court Says Business Can't Use Christian Symbol," reported by Fellowship of Companies for Christ, Atlanta.

[23]James C. Hefley, Lecture "How the Mass Media Influences Our Lives."

[24]Eric Mink: "Turner Abortion Show to Run as Scheduled," St. Louis Post-Dispatch, July 19, 1989, p. 31.

[25]As reported by Christian writers James C. Hefley and Edward E. Plowman in their book, Washington: Christians in the Corridors of Power, Tyndale House, 1975, pp. 40-42.

[26]"How the Mass Media Influences Our Lives," Op. Cit.

[27]Have I seen all of these films? No! But I have read reviews. You need not walk into a sewer. When smelling is sufficient.

[28]Peter S. Prescott: "Inside the Mind of a Murderer," Newsweek, April 23, 1990, p. 71.

[29]Newsweek, Op. Cit. p. 72.

[30]Even the Reader's Digest Condensed Books have come to present living together before marriage as normal.

[31]Rochunga Pudaite: The Greatest Book Ever Written,

Hannibal Books, 1989, p. 105.

[32]Washington: Christians in the Corridors of Power, Op. Cit., p. 46.

[33]Charles Colson and Daniel Van Ness: Convicted, Crossway Books, Westchester, IL, 1988, pp. 9, 13.

[34]James C. Hefley: Textbooks on Trial, Victor Books, Wheaton, IL, 1976, p. 15.

[35]Ibid, p. 57.

[36]Telecast over CBS-TV Network, June 15, 1980.

[37]"Man Denied Benefits Because of His Belief," Concerned Women for America Report, June, 1989, Vol. 11, No. 6, p. 18.

[38]John W. Whitehead: "Religious Liberty on Trial," Moody Monthly, November, 1988, pp. 20-23.

[39]Personal Interview, Wisconsin Concerned Women for America State Convention.

[40]James S. Robb: "Don Wildmon: The Methodist The Networks Love to Hate," Good News, September/October, 1989, p. 16.

[41]Donald E. Wildmon with Randall Nulton: Don Wildmon: The Man The Networks Love to Hate, Bristol Books, Wilmore, KY., 1989.

[42]For more information see: The Home Invaders by Victor Books, Wheaton, IL., 1985 and Don Wildmon: The Man the Networks Love to Hate, Bristol Books, Wilmore, Ky., 1989.

[43]"CleaR-TV Boycott: What's The Score?" Focus on the Family Citizen, March, 1990, p. 12.

[44]Tim Stafford: "His Father's Son," Christianity Today, April 22, 1988, pp. 16-22.

[45]Focus on the Family mailing, August, 1989, p. 7..

[46]Neil Eskelin: Pat Robertson, a Biography, Huntington

House, Lafayette, Louisiana, 1987, p. 179.

[47]Ibid, p. 24.

[48]Robert L. Koenig: "Putting a Lid On," St. Louis Post-Dispatch, November 6, 1989, pp. 1, 6.

[49]Dr. Ross Campbell with Pat Likes: How to Really Know Your Child and The Christian Family and Drugs, published by Victor Books, Wheaton, Illinois.

[50]Mel and Norma Gabler: What Are They Teaching Our Children? Victor Books, Wheaton, IL., 1985 pp. 164-173.

[51]"Doctors Warn TV a Danger," The Nashville Tennessean, April 17, 1990.

[52]Mike Royko: "Turn Off the TV, Tune in the Kids," St. Louis Post-Dispatch, April 19, 1990, p. 6F.

[53]National Association of 'Religious Broadcasters Convention, Washington, D.C., February, 1983.

[54]"Musicians Sing Out on 'Censors,'" St. Louis Post Dispatch, September 26, 1989, p. 4A.

[55]"Tolerant' Liberals Give In To Censorship," St. Louis Post Dispatch, September 17, 1989, p. 3B.

[56]"Decay in Values Led to Drug Problem," St. Louis Post Dispatch, September 13, 1989, p. 3c.

[57]"Prison Fellowship Comforts the Dying," St. Louis Post Dispatch, August 18, 1989, p. 3B.

[58]"Women's Magazines Push Pro-Choice Line," St. Louis Post Dispatch, August 22, 1989, p. 3B.

[59]"Beware Journalists With Secret Agendas," St. Louis Post Dispatch, October 18, 1989, p. 3C.

[60]Joy Publishing, 18320 Mt. Baldy Circle, Fountain Valley, CA 92708.

[61]Robert L. Slimp: "Oklahoma State University Regents 'Chief Quits Over 'The Last Temptation of Christ,' Christian News, November 6, 1989, p. 8.Dispatch, Sep-

tember 13, 1989, p. 3C.

[62]K. Jay and A. Young: "The Gay Report: Lesbians and Gay Men Speak Out About Their Sexual Experience and Lifestyles," Summit, New York, 1977.

[63]Article by Jean Seligmann, p. 39.

[64]"Truth in Labeling Goes for Press, Too," St. Louis Post Dispatch, October 31, 1989, p. 3B.

[65]Crossways Books, Westchester, IL, p. 78.

[66]"The New Political Power: The Evangelical Reporter," Focus on the Family Citizen, December, 1988, pp. 1, 2.

[67]"Robertson Forms New Grassroots Political Coalition," Word & Way, May 3, 1990, p. 16.

[68]"The Case of the Crusading Sheriff," Contact, April 4, 1964, pp. 1-4.

[69]Quoted from the Fond du Lac Reporter.

[70]Comments provided by Jack Clayton to Congressmen on possible applications of provisions in the Civil Rights Restoration Act. Also "Statement on Misinformation that Led to the Passage of the Grove City Bill," American Association of Christian Schools, 1988.

[71]Taken from Jimmy Draper: "From My Heart to Yours," Newsletter, First Baptist Church, Euless, TX., May 2, 1990, p. 2.

[72]Cervantes: Don Quixote, II. iv.

[73]Search for Freedom: America and Its People, The Macmillan Company, 1973, pp. 385-386.

[74]"Letters from the People," St. Louis Post-Dispatch, May 3, 1990, p. 2C.

[75]These and other questions and answers relating to the pro-life movement are included in "Pro-life Zingers and Sound Bites," Focus on the Family Citizen, May 21, 1990, pp. 12-15.

[76]Five Thousand Quotations for All Occasions, Edited by

Lewis C. Henry, Doubleday & Company, 1945, p. 191.

[77]"Take Gospel to the Heathen—Here and There," <u>Baptist Standard</u>, January 24, 1990, p. 6.

[78]"Church to Retain Status," <u>St. Louis Post-Dispatch</u>, May 1, 1989.

[79]Frank York: "Homosexual Militants Invade the Pews," <u>Focus on the Family Citizen</u>, March, 1990, pp. 1-3.

[80]Gustav Spohn: "Many Open, Practicing Gays are Ordained in Episcopal Church Since '77," Religious News Service. Reported in <u>Christian News</u>, January 22, 1990, pp. 1, 7.

[81]Gustav Spohn: "Kenyan Bishop Opposed to Homosexuality is 'Disinvited' by the Episcopalians," Religious News Service, May 22, 1990.

[82]Quoted from: <u>America: One Nation Under God</u>, Op. Cit.

GLOSSARY OF POLITICAL TERMS

Absentee ballot: A ballot cast by a registered voter who is unable to vote on election day. The absentee voter may vote by mail or at the county courthouse.

Advance personnel: A team that works ahead of the candidate on the campaign trail.

Affirmative Action: A policy of preferential hiring of minorities and women to insure nondiscrimination.

Apathy: A lack of voter interest in a political contest or local referendum.

Balanced ticket: A slate of party candidates, who by representing a variety of geographic regions, cultures, or religious backgrounds, can provide broader voter appeal.

Bandwagon: The tendency of people to "jump on board" a political campaign when it becomes obvious that a candidate will receive a large majority.

Bellwether: A state or district that takes the lead in indicating the voter turnout for a candidate or issue across the country.

Bipartisan: A candidate or issue that is acceptable to two parties.

Blanket primaries: An election in which candidates for the same office are listed on an election ballot without regard to party.

Campaign: A systematic effort to win an election mounted by a candidate or a political party.

Candidate appeal: Public perception of the personality, popularity, and past achievements of a candidate.

Caucus: A meeting (usually closed) that is held by local members of a political party (usually the leaders) to nominate candidates and determine policy.

Categorical: An unqualified and unconditional statement or denial of some alleged position or incident by a political candidate or elected official.

Closed primaries: An election for the nomination of candidates in which only party members may vote.

Coat tails: The increase in voter appeal that comes to a candidate by association with another candidate who has a greater following.

Conservative: One who seeks to preserve the existing political, social, or economic institutions of traditions and values.

Credentials committee: The group at a political convention that decides which delegates may participate in convention actions.

Crossover voter: A member of one political party who "crosses over" and votes for another party's candidates in an open primary.

Dark horse: A nominee or candidate about whom very little is known, or someone who unexpectedly wins an election.

Direct primary: An election within a political party in which voters select the party's candidates for the general election.

Districting: The way in which the population is divided to provide proportional representation in government.

Dyed-in-the-wool: A person who is steadfast in loyalty to a cause, candidate, or party.

Electoral college: A group of persons chosen by voters to formally elect the president and vice-president of the United States. The number in each state is determined by the state's population.

Exit poll: A survey of voters as they emerge from voting places to determine how the various candidates and issues are faring.

False association: A propaganda technique that falsely identifies a political candidate with a despicable cause or person.

Fat cat: A wealthy political contributor who has a record of contributing large sums to a party, candidate, or campaign.

Federal Election Commission: An official body, composed of Republicans and Democrats, who enforce federal election law and administer the public financing programs available to candidates.

Field manager: A person who coordinates the campaign efforts for a candidate, party, or issue within a particular area.

Follow the crowd: A propaganda technique that urges voters to join a perceived majority who are supporting a candidate or issue.

Front runner: A candidate among a group of candidates who seems most likely to win an election.

Gerrymander: To redraw election districts, made necessary by population growth or shifts, for the purpose of partisan advantage.

Glittering generality: A propaganda technique that uses a high-sounding phrase with little substance to sway opinions.

Grassroots interest group: A group of individuals at the local level who share common beliefs in a combined effort to influence government policy.

Incumbent: The holder of an office.

Lame duck: An officeholder whose influence and power is limited because he is not planning to run again, or is not eligible for reelection.

Liberal: A person who is seeking significant change in a society's political, social, or economic institutions; one who is tolerant and accepting of deviations from social and moral norms.

Mandate: The will of a large percentage of voters as expressed to their representatives.

Name calling: A propaganda technique that applies a strongly negative label, in an attempt to discredit a person or policy.

Nonpartisan: A candidate or issue not tied to the politics of any party.

Nomination by petition: A process of collecting the necessary number of signatures of registered voters required to place a candidate's name on an election ballot.

Open primaries: An election for nomination of candidates in which registered voters may cast ballots without making a public declaration of party afflication.

PACs: Political action committees organized to provide support to candidates and parties.

Partisanship: Firm and unwavering support of a candidate, party, or cause.

Plain folks: A propaganda technique that presents a candidate's ideas as good because he belongs to the common people.

Platform: A political party's policy statements on the issues believed of public concern during an election. The platform is prepared with an eye to uniting party factions by winning the support of various interests.

Plurality: The excess of votes received by the leading candidate over votes received by the next contender in an election with three or more candidates.

Political machine: An organized group of persons who control the operations of a political party.

Poll watchers: People who oversee a polling place during an election to ensure fair voting procedures.

Pragmatism: A practical rather than an ideological approach to politics.

Pork barrel: Government appropriations voted by legislators for non-essential projects in their districts. Intended to ingratiate legislators with their constitutents. Pork barrel amendments in Congress are frequently attached to desirable legislation so as to improve chances of adoption.

Precinct: A district in a county or city in which voters within a prescribed geographical area vote.

Pressure group: A special interest group which attempts to influence legislation and changes in government policy.

Proportional representation: A system employed in a defined governmental area (nation, state, county, etc.) designed so that each legislator is representing approximately the same number of constitutents.

Rank and file: The members of a political party or organization.

Shoo-in: A candidate who is regarded as certain to win an election.

Single member district: A district that elects only one
representative to the state legislature.

Single issue election: A contest in which an election is
decided by candidate positions on a single issue, rather
than on overall ideology. The critical issue may vary
from one district and state to another.

Splinter group: An organization formed by disaffected
members of a political party.

Stacking the deck: Selective use of words and facts to
give a false or misleading perception of a candidate or a
party's record and positions on issues. Using this
propaganda technique, a political activist will use half
truths and other deceptive rhetoric to make out the best
case for his side and the worst case for his opponent's.

Straight ticket: The manner in which a person votes for
all the candidates on a ballot nominated by one political
party.

Standard bearer: The candidate who is running for the
most important office in an election. In a presidential
election year, the standard bearer for a party is the
party's candidate for president.

Straw poll: An informal, non-scientific survey of public
opinion.

Testimonial: A propaganda technique that tries to win
voter acceptance of a candidate or an idea through the
endorsement of a movie star, sports personality, or some
other celebrity.

Ticket splitting: Voting for candidates of different parties on a ballot.

Trial balloon: An idea that is released to the media by a
political operative or candidate to test the reaction of
public opinion.

Underdog: The candidate least favored to win in an election.

Watch dog committee: A group of citizens who oversees what politicans and public officials do.

RESOURCE AGENCIES FOR A BETTER AMERICA

ABORTION, INFANTICIDE, AND EUTHANSASIA

Americans Against Abortion Box 70, Lindale, TX 75771-0070. (214)-963-8671.
Produces pro-life tracts, videos, posters, and advertisements.

American Life League Inc. PO Box 1350, Stafford, VA 22554 (703)-659-4171.
Publishes monthly magazine, supplies documented information to local groups fighting abortion.

American Portrait Films 1695 W. Crescent Avenue, Suite 500, Anaheim, CA 92801.
Produces and distributes conscience-awakening films, including "The Silent Scream," "A Matter of Choice," and "Conceived in Liberty."

American Rights Coalition PO Box 487, Chattanooga, TN 37405 (800)-634-2224.
Assistance for women injured by abortion. Files suit in cases of medical malpractice.

Americans United for Life, 343 S. Dearborn, Suite 1804, Chicago, IL 60604 (312)-786-9494.

Boca Raton Christian Action Council PO Box 2644, Boca Raton, FL 33427.
Offers a 305-page "Resource Manual" for those fighting the horrors of abortion. $10 donation per copy.

Christian Action Council 701 West Broad Street, Suite 405, Falls Church, VA 22046 (703)-237-2100
Provides instructions for opening a crisis pregnancy center.

Christian Life Commission of the Southern Baptist Convention 901 Commerce Street, Suite 550, Nashville, TN 37203 (615)-244-2355.
Offers a number of inexpensive, well-written, Biblically-fortressed books on abortion and pro-life concerns.

Focus on the Family PO Box 500, Pomona, CA 91799.
Has a wealth of family-related resources with a pro-life emphasis, including Focus on the Family Citizen (one-year membership $15) and Focus on the Family Physician (one-year membership $20).

Human Life Foundation 150 E. 35th St. New York, NY 10016.

Legal Action for Women 1145 Candlewood Circle Pensacola, FL 32514 (904)-474-1091.
Offers legal counsel, files malpractice suites. Provides radio and TV spots.

Methodists for Life 12105 Livingston St., Wheaton, MD 20902 (301)-942-1627.
Offers special help for United Methodists involved in pro-life concerns and for changing pro-choice policies in denominational bureaucracies.

Minnesota Citizens Concerned for Life 4249 Nicollet Avenue, Minneapolis, MN 55409 (612)-825-6831.
Offers books, brochures, slide sets, cassettes, videos, fetal models, stickers, lapel roses, buttons, and many other aids in fighting abortion.

National Right to Life Committee Suite 500, 419 7th Street, NW Washington, DC 20004 (202)-626-8800.

Operation Rescue PO Box 1180, Binghamton, New York 13902.
Because of their intervention to prevent the killing of unborn babies, many OR members are now in jail. Has available a variety of video and audio cassettes, and literature. The story of Operation Rescue, published by Whitaker House is available from OR or your local

Christian book store. Another good OR book is <u>90 Days for Life</u>, the jailhouse journal of Rev. Fred Kerr who was arrested in Atlanta for participating in an OR intervention. Order this book for $7.95 plus $2 shipping from Hannibal Books, 921 Center St., Hannibal, MO 63401. Also available in many Christian bookstores.

Presbyterians for Life PO Box 953, Decatur, GA 30031.
A pro-life organization for Presbyterian ministers and laity.

Pro-Life Action League 6160 North Cicero Avenue, Chicago, IL 60646 (312)-777-2900.
Trains "sidewalk counselors" for pro-life ministry.

Pro-Life Direct Action League PO Box 11881, St. Louis, MO 63105 (314)-863-1022.
Nondenominational. Dedicated to sanctity-of-life ethic and the rescue of unborn children.

Sanctity of Life Ministries 4941 Oriskany Dr., Annandale, VA 22003 (703)-256-5433.

AIDS

Love and Action 3 Church Circle, Annapolis, MD 21401 (301)-268-3442.
Volunteer ministry serving people with AIDS, their families, friends, and churches. Provides an AIDS education program for churches.

Victory House 719 SW 4th Court, Fort Lauderdale, FL 33312 (305)-463-0848.
Provides housing for people with AIDS and counseling for those desiring freedom from homosexuality.

ALCOHOLISM/DRUG INTERVENTION

Alcoholics for Christ 1316 North Campbell Road, Royal Oak, MI 48067 (800)-441-7877.
Nondenominational, nonprofit, evangelical fellowship for alcohol abusers and their families.

International Union of Gospel Missions PO Box 10780, Kansas City, MO 64118 (800)-624-5156.
A worldwide association of rescue ministries, providing materials, training, and assistance to urban missions.

Salvation Army National Headquarters 799 Bloomfield Avenue Verona, NJ 07044 (201)-239-0606.
International Christian charitable movement that provides personal spiritual counseling and physical help to all in need.

Teen Challenge 1525 North Campbell Avenue, Springfield, MO 65803 (417)-862-2781.

Walter Hoving Home for Women PO Box 194, Garrison, NY 10524 (914)-424-3674.
A one-year school promoting Christian growth for substance abusing women 18-55.

CAMPUS OUTREACH

Campus Crusade For Christ Arrowhead Springs, San Bernardino, CA 92414 (714)-886-5224.
Interdenominational ministry of evangelism and discipleship.

Fellowship of Christian Athletes 8701 Leeds Road, Kansas City, MO 64129 (800)-289-0909.
Volunteer group of athletes offering Bible-based spiritual nurturing to school athletes.

InterVarsity Christian Fellowship 6400 Schroeder Road, PO Box 7895 Madison, WI 53707-7895 (608)-274-9001.
Publishes Christian books for thinking readers. Sponsors IV chapters for nurturing and discipling of college students.

The Navigators PO Box 6000, Colorado Springs, CO 80934 (719)-598-1212.
Campus ministries focusing on evangelism and discipleship.

Young Life PO Box 520 720 West Monument, Colorado Springs, CO 80901 (719)-473-4262.
Senior and junior high school relational ministry. Sponsors student meetings, week-long summer camps and seminary-level Institute for Youth Ministers.

Youth For Christ PO Box 419, Wheaton, IL 60189 (312)-668-6600.
International ministry on high school campuses. Provides short-term missions for teens through Project Serve.

Youth With A Mission Box 296, Sunland, CA 91040 (818)-896-2755.
Short term mission opportunities in many nations.

CRISIS PREGNANCY/ABORTION ALTERNATIVES

Birthright 777 Coxwell Avenue, Toronto, Canada M4C 3C6 (800)-328-LOVE.
Operates nearly 600 crisis pregnancy centers in the United States and Canada.

Bethany Christian Services 901 Eastern Avenue NE, Grand Rapids, MI 49503 (616)-459-6269 (Office) (800)-238-4269 (Hotline).
Evangelical adoption agency.

Christian Maternity Home Association C/O Loving and Caring 1817 Olde Homestead Lane, Suite H, Lancaster, PA 17601 (717)-293-3230.
Helps groups start maternity homes. Can write state licensing manuals, help train staff, provide consultation and program review. Publishes annual directory.

Liberty Godparent Ministries PO Box 2700, Lynchburg, VA 24506 (804)-384-3043 (Office) 1-800-368-3336 (Hotline).

Loving and Caring Inc. 1817 Olde Homestead Lane, Lancaster, PA 17601 (717)-293-3230.
Trains host couples for women with crisis pregnancies;

offers counseling, retreats and seminars; publishes counseling materials.

New Beginnings 40 25th Avenue North, St. Cloud, MN 56303 (612)-255-1252.
Home for single pregnant women. Self-help program providing professional counseling and support services.

DECENCY IN PUBLIC LIFE

American Family Association PO Drawer 2440, Tupelo, MS 38803 601-844-5036.
Promotes decency in TV and other media. Encourages biblical, pro-family, and traditional values.

Mastermedia International Inc. 2102 Palm Avenue, Highland, CA 92346 (714)-864-5250.
Ministry of evangelization and discipleship to film and TV leaders. Provides information to the Christian community about media-related issues.

Morality in Media 475 Riverside Drive, New York, NY 10115 (212)-870-3222.
National organization to stop pornography through education and vigorous enforcement of laws. Provides legal information to prosecutors and other interested attorneys.

National Coalition Against Pornography 800 Compton Road, Suite 9224, Cincinnati, OH 45231 (513)-512-6227.
Alliance of citizens, religious groups and private organizations to eliminate hard-core pornography through education and legal action. Offers educational materials.

Parents' Music Resource Center 1500 Arlington Boulevard, Suite 330, Arlington, VA 22209 (703)-527-9466.
Educates consumers about violent, pornographic, and pro-drug messages in popular music.

HANDICAPPED

Broken Wing Outreach 3361 Republic Avenue, Minneapolis, MN 55426 (612)-920-8147.
Provides Bible studies, retreats, concerts, worship services, and programs for the physically disabled.

Christian Horizons PO Box 334, Williamston, MI 48895 (517)-655-3463.
Interdenominational ministry to mentally handicapped. Assists churches in identifying persons with special needs.

Christian League for the Handicapped PO Box 948, Walworth, WI 53184 (414)-275-6131.
Residency, employment, camping, and outreach for physically disabled adults.

Joni and Friends Handicap Ministries PO Box 333, Agoura Hills, CA 91301 (818)-707-5664.
Links disabled people with the local church through evangelism, inspiration, and discipline.

HOMOSEXUALITY INTERVENTION

Exodus International PO Box 2121, San Rafael, CA 94912-2121 (415)-454-1017.
Clearinghouse for Christ-centered ministries to those overcoming homosexuality and other life-dominating sexual problems. Provides information on over 60 national ministries.

Homosexuals Anonymous Fellowship Services Box 7881 Reading, PA 19603 (800)-253-3000.
Provides group support and a 14-step recovery program.

HOSPICE/NURSING HOME MINISTRY

Love Thy Neighbor Box 386, Camby, OR 97013 (503)-678-2228.

LEGAL DEFENSE AND RECONILIATION

Association of Christian Conciliation Services PO Box 1492, Merrifield, VA 22116 (703)-642-1070.
Helps Christians who are odds with one another to reconcile relationships and resolve disputes before a panel of believers rather than secular courts.

National Legal Foundation 6477 College Park Square, Suite 306, Virginia Beach, VA 23464 (804)-424-4242.
Nonprofit law firm dedicated to the restoration and defense of Constitutional freedoms, with primary emphasis on the First Amendment.

Rutherford Institute PO Box 510, Manassas, VA 22110 (703)-369-0100.
Nonprofit legal and educational organization specializing in the defense of religious freedom, sanctity of human life and family autonomy.

LITERACY TRAINING

The Contact Literacy Center PO Box 81826, Lincoln, NE 68501-1826 (800)-228-8813.
Secular, international information and referral service. Also links prisoners and ex-prisoners with community resources for jobs, housing and other service.

Literacy Volunteers of America 5795 Widewaters Parkway, Syracuse, NY 13214 (315)-445-8000.
Secular, national nonprofit literacy training organization networking through volunteer programs.

MILITARY

Christian Military Fellowship PO Box 1207, Englewood, CO 80150 (303)-761-1959.
Evangelical association providing spiritual, educational, and personal support to American military personnel and their families.

Navigators PO Box 6000, Colorado Springs, CO 80934 (719)-598-1212.
Worldwide evangelism and discipleship materials to help military personnel apply Scripture to everyday life.

Overseas Christian Servicemen's Centers PO Box 1268, Englewood, CO 80150 (303)-762-1400.
Evangelization and discipleship for military personnel and their families.

NEIGHBORHOOD/FRIENDSHIP EVANGELISM

Adult Christian Education Foundation PO Box 8398, Madison, WI 53708 (608)-849-5933.
Assists local churches in serious Bible study. Brochure available.

Neighborhood Bible Study PO Box 222, Dobbs Ferry, NY 10522 (914)-963-3273.
Assists individuals and churches in starting neighborhood Bible study groups.

PRISON MINISTRIES

Bill Glass Evangelistic Association PO Box 356, Dallas, TX 75221 (214)-291-7895.
Conducts "Total Person Weekends" in state and federal prisons.

Good News Jail And Prison Ministry 1036 South Highland Street, Arlington, VA 22204 (703)-979-2200
Trains and places full-time prison chaplains. Ministers to prison staffs, inmates, and families.

International Prison Ministry PO Box 63, Dallas, TX 75221 (800)-527-1212.
Provides Bibles and study helps in Spanish and English.

Prison Fellowship Ministries PO 17500, Washington, DC 20041-0500 (703)-478-0100.
Founded by converted Watergate figure Charles Colson. Ministry to prisoners, ex-prisoners, and families.

Prison Mission Association PO Box 3397, Riverside, CA 92519-3397 (714)-686-2613.
Conducts Bible Correspondence Fellowship and ministers to military.

Yokefellows International Prison Ministry 1200 Almond Street, Williamsport, PA 17701 (717)-326-6868.
Conducts weekly dialogues on Christian themes in over 300 prisons and jails.

PUBLIC ADVOCACY GROUPS

Concerned Women for America 122 C Street NW, Suite, 800 Washington, DC 20001.
An effective pro-family, pro-life organization that promotes traditional moral values, religious freedom, free enterprise, a strong national defense, and trains volunteer lobbyists and provides legal defense for defendants endeavoring to protect their First Amendment rights. I have been personally active in CWA for many years and recommend this organization highly.

Eagle Forum PO Box 618, Alton, IL 62002 (618)-462-5415.
A pro-family organization that promotes traditional moral values, patriotism, private enterprise, and a strong national defense.

Family Research Council 601 Pennsylvania Avenue NW, Suite 901, Washington, DC 20004 (202)-393-2100.
Research and lobbying division of Focus on the Family, encouraging traditional Judeo-Christian family values in government decisions.

Focus on the Family PO Box 500, Pomona, CA 91799 (714)-620-8500.
Family broadcast ministry which also publishes magazines that report on legislation, the media, education trends and decency issues.

Heritage Foundation 214 Massachusetts Ave., N.E., Washington, DC 20002 (213)-382-2156.
Highly respected "think tank" advocating free

enterprise, limited government, individual liberty, and a strong national defense.

Institute on Religion and Democracy 729 15th Street NW Suite 900 Washington, DC 20005 (202)-393-3200.
Broad-based programs supporting religious liberty and democratic institutions around the world. Produces educational material foreign policy; critiques imbalanced and radical public policy within religious denominations.

National Association of Evangelicals 1023 15th Street NW Suite 500 Washington, DC 20005 (202)-789-1011.
Washington lobbying group representing evangelical views on governmental issues and First Amendment concerns. Publishes a periodic report.

The Roundtable P.O. Box 11467, 3295 Poplar Ave, Memphis, TN 38111 (901) 458-3795.
A coalition of political, business, military, and religious leaders, whose focus is on public policy concerning moral issues.

RELIEF/DEVELOPMENT

Christian Children's Fund PO Box 26511, Richmond, VA 23219.
Individual sponsors care for children and their families in 28 nations. Services include education, medical and dental care, food, clothing and shelter. Emphasis is on eventual self help.

Food for the Hungry 7729 East Greenway Road, Scottsdale, AZ 85260 (800)-2HUNGER.
International Christian relief and development agency meeting both physical and spiritual hunger. Seeks volunteers for overseas short-term and long-term work through Hunger Corps.

Project Mercy 7011 Ardmore Avenue, Fort Wayne, IN 46809 (219)-747-2559.
Food, clothing, and financial assistance provided for

African refugees. American volunteers sew African-style clothing for overseas distribution.

Samaritan's Purse PO Box 3000, Route 4, Bamboo Road Boone, NC 28607 (704)-262-1980.
Meets emergency needs among missionaries, national church leaders and the people they serve.

World Emergency Relief 530 Monte Vista Avenue, PO Box 977, Glendale, CA 91209 818-242-4782.
Provides food and medicine to disaster victims in Africa and the Caribbean. Conducts radio evangelism and crusades.

World Relief PO Box WRC, Wheaton, IL 60189 (800)-535-LIFE.
Provides worldwide emergency relief and development programs.

World Vision 919 West Huntington Drive, Monrovia, CA 91016 (818)-357-7979.
Child-care, relief, and development agency operating more than 5,000 projects in 80-plus countries.

SCHOOLS, EDUCATION, BETTER TEXTBOOKS

Christian Educators Association International PO Box 50025, Pasadena, CA 91105 (818)-798-1124.
Helpful to Christian educators in public and private schools. Encourages Christian educators. Offers information for parent-action groups, legal advice, counsel, and curriculum materials.

Citizens for Educational Freedom Rosslyn Plaza, Suite 805, 1611 N. Kent St., Arlington, VA 22209 (703)-524-1991.
Promotes local control of public schools and respect for religious and moral values of parents and children. Provides options for released-time religious instruction and promotes educational vouchers for parents who choose to send their children to non-government schools.

Citizens for Excellence in Education Box 3200, Costa Mesa, CA 92628 (714)-546-5931.
A division of the National Association of Christian Educators (same address as above). Promotes better education in academics and moral and spiritual values in public schools.

Educational Research Analysts PO Box 7518, Longview, TX 65601.
Headed by Mel and Norma Gabler, this is the most successful agency in America for getting better textbooks into public schools. Offers books, reviews, and step-by-step directions for becoming involved in textbook selection in your child's schools.

SERVICE NETWORK

Love Inc. PO Box 1616, Holland, MI 49422 (616)-392-8277.
Local chapters link needy individuals and families with church outreach programs and services.

SEX EDUCATION

Respect Inc. PO Box 349, Bradley, IL 60915 (815)-932-8389.
Provides sex education materials with a Christian slant for public junior and senior high schools.

Teen-Aid North 1330 Calispel, Spokane, WA 99201 (509)-328-2080.
Materials for parent workshops and senior and junior high curricula. Encourages abstinence, role modeling, and strong family ties.

Josh McDowell Ministry PO Box 1000, Dallas, TX 75221 (214)-907-1000.
"Why Wait?" campaign encourages teens to resist sexual pressure. Presents positive reasons for waiting until marriage.

TROUBLED YOUTH

Youth for Christ Youth Guidance Division 360 Main Place, Carol Stream, Il 60188 (312)-668-6600.
Nation's largest evangelical outreach to juvenile offenders. Works with juvenile courts, probation departments, and police. Will help set up local chapter and train full-time staff.

VOLUNTEERS FOR HELPING THE NEEDY

Habitat for Humanity Habitat and Church Streets, Americus, GA 31709 (912)-924-6935.
International ministry dependent on volunteer labor to plan and build housing for poor families. Former President Jimmy Carter is a supporter and volunteer.

Roving Volunteers in Christ's Service 1499 Edgewood Ranch Road, Orlando, FL 32811 (407)-293-4170.
Retired couples travel in their RV's (recreation vehicles) to a new building or maintenance project every three or four weeks.

Please send me:

We Can Change America . . . and Here's How" by Darylann Whitemarsh. How to make things happen in the public arena. Especially helpful for pro-lifers to use in coming battles to save the unborn.

_____ Copies at $9.95 = _____

The Truth in Crisis, The Controversy in the Southern Baptist Convention

Volume 1	_____ Copies at $7.95 = _____
Volume 2	_____ Copies at $7.95 = _____
Volume 3	_____ Copies at $7.95 = _____
Volume 4	_____ Copies at $8.95 = _____
Volume 5	_____ Copies at $8.95 = _____

Guilty Until Proven Innocent by Keith Barnhart with Lila Shelburne. Dramatic true story of the prosecution of an innocent pastor charged with sexual child abuse. A must book for all who work with children.

_____ Copies at $9.95 = _____

90 Days for Life by Fred Kerr. A spiritual journal by a minister in jail for protesting abortion.

_____ Copies at $7.95 = _____

Where Is God When a Child Suffers? by Penny Giesbrecht. How a Christian family copes with their child's pain in the light of God's love.

_____ Copies at $8.95 = _____

The Greatest Book Ever Written by Dr. Rochunga Pudaite with James C. Hefley, Ph.D. Praised by evangelical leaders as an outstanding apologetic on the Bible.

_____ Copies at $9.95 = _____

Please add $2.00 postage and handling for first book, plus .50 for each additional book.

Shipping & Handling _____

MO residents add sales tax _____

TOTAL ENCLOSED (Check or money order) _____

Name _____

Address _____

City _____ State ___ Zip_____ Phone _____

MAIL TO HANNIBAL BOOKS, 921 Center, Hannibal, MO 63401. Satisfaction guaranteed. Call 314-221-2462 for quantity prices.

Please send me:

We Can Change America . . . and Here's How" by Darylann Whitemarsh. How to make things happen in the public arena. Especially helpful for pro-lifers to use in coming battles to save the unborn.
_____ Copies at $9.95 = _____

The Truth in Crisis, The Controversy in the Southern Baptist Convention
Volume 1   _____ Copies at $7.95 = _____
Volume 2   _____ Copies at $7.95 = _____
Volume 3   _____ Copies at $7.95 = _____
Volume 4   _____ Copies at $8.95 = _____
Volume 5   _____ Copies at $8.95 = _____

Guilty Until Proven Innocent by Keith Barnhart with Lila Shelburne. Dramatic true story of the prosecution of an innocent pastor charged with sexual child abuse. A must book for all who work with children.
_____ Copies at $9.95 = _____

90 Days for Life by Fred Kerr. A spiritual journal by a minister in jail for protesting abortion.
_____ Copies at $7.95 = _____

Where Is God When a Child Suffers? by Penny Giesbrecht. How a Christian family copes with their child's pain in the light of God's love.
_____ Copies at $8.95 = _____

The Greatest Book Ever Written by Dr. Rochunga Pudaite with James C. Hefley, Ph.D. Praised by evangelical leaders as an outstanding apologetic on the Bible.
_____ Copies at $9.95 = _____

Please add $2.00 postage and handling for first book, plus .50 for each additional book.
Shipping & Handling   _____
MO residents add sales tax _____

TOTAL ENCLOSED (Check or money order) _____

Name _____

Address _____

City _____ State ___ Zip_____ Phone _____

MAIL TO HANNIBAL BOOKS, 921 Center, Hannibal, MO 63401. Satisfaction guaranteed. Call 314-221-2462 for quantity prices.